As a father of three daughters, I could not put this boo Every page is practical, inspiring, and life-changing. Pam and Doreen are the perfect people to take you on this rite-of-passage journey with your daughters. If you follow their advice, your girls will literally be transformed.

—JIM BURNS, Ph.D., President, HomeWord, Author of *Teaching Your Children Healthy Sexuality*

Attention all moms and mentors: Do not pass by this book! This is an opportunity to have your daughter come into the fullness of being a true Modern-Day Princess.

—PATSY CLAIRMONT, Women of Faith speaker, Author of *Kaleidoscope*

This book is long overdue. For years, mothers have asked me if there was a resource or book that would aid them in guiding their daughters through the rite of passage from girlhood to womanhood. I can't wait to tell them that help is on the way! Bravo to Pam and Doreen for meeting the need!

—VICKI COURTNEY, Best-selling author of *Your Girl* and *5 Conversations You Must Have With Your Daughter*

I have always said that it's better to build children than to repair adults. However, much of my ministry centers on healing women's broken hearts and mending shattered dreams. Finally, we have a resource that focuses on prevention rather than repair. Pam Farrel and Doreen Hanna have crafted an invaluable resource in *Raising a Modern-Day Princess,* to help moms and dads encourage and equip young teens to avoid the common mistakes that lead to future pain. Through mature mentoring, godly guidance, and biblical truth, their seven-week program helps girls realize their true identity as daughters of the King and move into adulthood abundantly prepared. This book is for every parent or mentor who longs for young girls to walk into their future with the courage and confidence of princesses who know they are deeply loved, tenderly treasured, and divinely designed.

—SHARON JAYNES, International speaker and Author of *The Power of a Woman's Words*

In a very easy, readable format, Pam and Doreen unfold life-giving words to moms and dads on how they can instill grace, worth, dignity, inner beauty, and destiny into the lives of their daughters. Whether you implement one or all of the ideas in this book, you will find this book invaluable as you invest in the lives of your daughters.

—FERN NICHOLS, President/Founder, Moms In Touch International,
Author of *When Moms Pray Together*

We all live in a world with tremendous pressure on teen girls. In *Raising a Modern-Day Princess*, Pam Farrel and Doreen Hanna create a refreshing and helpful tool for parents and leaders to better equip and encourage tomorrow's wives, moms, and leaders by preparing today's teens. If you're a mom and you have a daughter . . . you need this book!

—JILL SAVAGE, Founder and CEO, Hearts at Home, Author of
Real Moms . . . Real Jesus

Raising a Modern-Day Princess is the resource I've been hoping to come across for years. Raising a girl in this day and age is a daunting task. In this book, Pam and Doreen answer the questions all moms of daughters are asking, and give solid, wise answers. If you've been looking for a handbook to help you raise your daughter according to biblical principles; you'll be overjoyed with this book.

—LYSA TERKEURST, President, Proverbs 31 Ministries, Speaker, Author of
Becoming More than a Good Bible Study Girl, and proud mom of three
modern-day princesses

The fairy tales will pass away but the Word of God will last forever. *Raising a Modern-Day Princess* reveals the truth of how God has called our girls to be His princesses. It is illustrated by the authors' tender care and wisdom of God's view of His daughters. Every girl should experience her rite of passage to become a princess, and every woman that guides her on this journey will be richly blessed.

—DR. THELMA WELLS, D.D., President, A Woman of God Ministries,
Speaker/Author/Founder of the Ready To Win Conferences

Raising a
Modern-Day
Princess

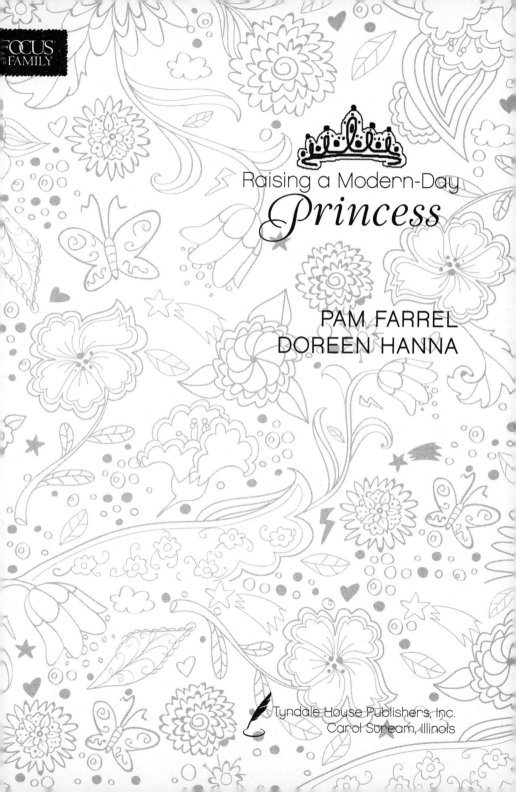

Raising a Modern-Day
Princess

PAM FARREL
DOREEN HANNA

Tyndale House Publishers, Inc.
Carol Stream, Illinois

Library of Congress Cataloging-in-Publication Data
Farrel, Pam, 1959-
   Raising a modern-day princess : inspiring purpose, value, and strength in your daughter / by Pam Farrel and Doreen Hanna.
      p. cm.
   "A Focus on the Family book."
   Includes bibliographical references.
   ISBN-13: 978-1-58997-574-3
   ISBN-10: 1-58997-574-X
   1. Mothers and daughters—Religious aspects—Christianity. 2. Parenting—Religious aspects—Christianity.
I. Hanna, Doreen. II. Title.
   BV4529.18.F37 2009
   248.8'45—dc22

                                                2009025337

Printed in the United States of America
4 5 6 7 8 9 / 15 14 13 12 11

To my husband, Chad, Honey, you have been my pillar
of strength and support as we have traveled to
mountaintop highs as well as some lonely valleys in this
journey. I am grateful that I can enjoy this pinnacle with you.

To my girls, Brandy Corea and Kamy Hanna, You were my
Aaron- and Hur-ettes! You both labored faithfully alongside
me in the early stages of writing the curriculum. Your
creative minds made it fun and engaging for every girl who
has participated. I could not have done this without you.

To my Shekinah Faith and Hannah Laynne,
Your Leila awaits the day that you will receive your
crown and then carry on this tradition in your own
families. I pray that you will touch the lives of the
generations that will follow you as you become
the leaders of Treasured Celebrations.

—DOREEN

To my granddaughter, Eden, and all my future grandchildren,
Nana wrote this so that one day you, too, will feel a crown
on your beautiful head and know that you are a daughter of
the King of Kings, a Modern-Day Princess. Walk worthy!

*To all the young women I have mentored and discipled over the
past 30-plus years,* You taught me much more than I taught
you. My life is better because you are in it.

To my sons, Brock, Zach, and Caleb, You are princes of men,
real Modern-Day Knights! Thank you for making wise
choices in the women you have brought into our
family or will bring into our family. Quality attracts
quality, so thanks for being quality men.

To Hannah, You are God's princess,
beautiful from the inside out!

To my precious husband, Bill, You teach men that if
"you treat your wife like a queen, she'll want to treat you
like a king." Well, my kingly husband, I love you! This and
every book I have written would never have been completed
without your encouragement and support. You are the best!

—PAM

Contents

Acknowledgments

First, I [Doreen] would like to acknowledge Chris Cannon, senior pastor of King's Harbor Church in Torrance, CA, and former youth pastor Kenny Keating for believing in this vision. Their affirmation was demonstrated by their immediate response to implement the first Daughter of the King class within our church and then undergird the ministry with financial support.

My deepest gratitude goes to Steve Arterburn for laying down his identical vision for teen girls and sending me out to pursue it. He continues today to show his support by standing as one of Treasured Celebrations Ministries' board members.

I would also like to recognize those who have been like the wind beneath my wings as they caught the vision and demonstrated their belief by opening doors for the ministry to be established and supporting its continued growth. Marlow Clemens secured Treasured Celebrations' 501(c)(3) status. Those who have been angels with skin on include Debi Leach, Sharon Barnes, Diane Maxey "Cookie" Currier, Anthony Naraducci, Jody Komae, Maggi Socea, Lorraine Gruys, Florence Littauer, Gary and Heather Hershberger, Evie Bailey, Christy Knoll Shannon, and The Light at Mission Viejo Missions Board. An extra-special acknowledgment goes to Larry Socea for editing the first attempts of this manuscript— what a true labor of love.

With joy overflowing I must sing high praises for those who continue to carry out this ministry by their commitment to be regional and national representatives for Treasured Celebrations Ministries. These women are also some of God's women warriors for our teenage girls today: Julie Hayes, Ontario, Canada; Naomi Shedd, Acworth, GA; Marissa

Perez, Southern CA; Stephanie Banda, South Bay, CA; and Kara Ash-baugh, my personal assistant and Santa Fe, NM, representative.

Treasured Celebrations Ministries acquired a local Santa Fe, New Mexico, advisory board in 2008. Their role has already strengthened the ministry locally and has helped raise a greater visibility in our local community and throughout the state of New Mexico. I pray that my depth of appreciation for each of you has been expressed through my words and actions.

Lastly, this book would not carry the quality of authorship without the loving mentorship of my co-author, Pam Farrel. What a mighty woman of God! She has touched the lives of millions, and yet God stirred her heart to come alongside me as she also caught the vision of this ministry years ago. Pam, you are one of my most treasured God-given gifts in this season of my life.

—DOREEN HANNA

Introduction

Someday you will be old enough
to start reading fairy tales again.

—C. S. Lewis

At some point in her life, almost every young woman longs to feel like a princess. Little girls play dress-up and pretend to be royalty. Most young women dream of a beautiful wedding where they can wear a white dress and, at least for one day, feel like a princess who is marrying her prince. Many of our girls today have grown up watching *Sleeping Beauty*, *Snow White and the Seven Dwarfs*, and *The Little Mermaid*—all stories of young women who were daughters of kings.

Just as Sleeping Beauty didn't know she was a princess, most young women today have yet to embrace their royal standing in Christ. They've yet to understand that they should see themselves as daughters of the King of Kings. God loves these young women, and it is our guess that because you are reading this book, you love a young woman, or several of them, and want to be a positive influence in her life.

When a young woman can hear, see, and feel the love of her Father in Heaven, she is changed. Just as a caterpillar emerges from a cocoon as a butterfly, a young woman can fly into womanhood in beauty and valor if we help her grasp the love of God. This journey into womanhood takes a team.

In the book of Esther, we see that this future queen had a group of dedicated and talented people around her preparing her for her first meeting with the king. In the same way, a young woman is more likely to be successful if she has a team around her that loves her, teaches her, trains her, and pours truth into her in a way that helps her grow into her "glass slippers."

Throughout this book, we will share our stories and the stories of many women, young and older, to help you see your role in helping create an army of Modern-Day Princesses. And if you are a male, you will learn more about your priceless, unique role in the life of a budding princess.

In each chapter, I [Pam] will share simple secrets to being a powerful, proactive mentor. I have been mentoring and discipling women of all ages for more than 30 years. When my own sons were pre-teens, I read Robert Lewis's book *Raising a Modern-Day Knight*. After reading that book, my husband and I elected to incorporate a rite of passage into our family life for our sons, a decision that has served them well. I also remember thinking, *There needs to be something like this for girls!* So I began to pray that God would place this burden and vision on the heart of a creative woman leader. I also continued to mentor young women and be Mom to my men, praying for the women they would someday marry. So far, God has led one of my three sons to an amazing Modern-Day Princess.

Even as Pam was praying for a woman to champion the need for a rite-of-passage experience for girls, God was preparing me [Doreen] to share my passion for helping young women realize their place as daughters of the King—true Modern-Day Princesses.

In June of 1999, I envisioned the amazing blessings and crowning moments to come after researching what it meant to be a daughter of the King—a princess in God's kingdom. In studying numerous cultures' ways to celebrate a girl's step into womanhood, I found that there was often a process, a journey to the moment when a daughter is crowned with that culture's sentiment of royalty. After reading these valuable, purpose-driven rite-of-passage rituals, my passion to see this happen for the Christian community was uncontainable. It was time to create!

The first curriculum developed was titled *Celebrate! You're a Daughter of the King* (referred to from here on out as DOK). In 2005, we renamed it *Becoming a Modern-Day Princess* (referred to from here on out as MDP). The MDP program also now provides a faith-based (10-session) and a community-based (7-session) curriculum that groups of girls can do together in preparation for a rite of passage, or moms and daughters can use one-on-one in preparation for a family rite-of-passage ceremony.

It has been, and still remains, my strongest desire to see every family celebrate their daughter's rite of passage into womanhood. When we know Christ as our Savior (enabling us to embrace God as our Heavenly Father), we are royalty, daughters and sons of the King. Therefore, in 2000, I, along with many other women who have caught this vision, began to teach and help our daughters understand the royalty they possess as they journey through their rite of passage and then celebrate their step into womanhood.

Courtside

Welcome to the royal court! Your place here is crucial to this generation and the generations to come. Young women await your wisdom, love, and energy so they, too, can step into the court of the King of Kings and claim their tiaras.

Those in the "court" of a future princess often include her mother, the women of her extended family, teachers, church or community youth workers, her pastor or youth pastor, a mentor, and her father or a father figure in her life. She longs to be affirmed, encouraged, and mentored by these people. Of primary importance to this young woman is the desire to hear the words of blessing from her earthly father so she can be trained to recognize the voice of her Father in Heaven.

She is in search of a blessing—words of deep, meaningful affirmation that will build her confidence and identity as a Modern-Day Princess. Throughout this book, we'll show you step-by-step how to give your daughter, or the young woman in your life, the affirmation and guidance she needs as she moves into adulthood. We'll give you ideas for ways to create a memorable rite-of-passage ceremony for the young woman or women you know. You *can* make a difference. You can influence generations to come and leave a lasting legacy of godly girls who become godly women, abundantly prepared to be difference makers. Ready to change the world, one princess at a time?

Seeking My Father's Blessing: What Every Young Woman Longs For

"I'll be a Father to you; you'll be sons and daughters to me."
The Word of the Master, God.

—2 CORINTHIANS 6:18 (MSG)

I am a princess. All girls are. Even if they live in tiny old attics;
even if they dress in rags; even if they aren't pretty,
or smart, or young. They're still princesses. All of us.
Didn't your father ever tell you that? Didn't he?

—A LITTLE PRINCESS (1995)

*L*ying in my bed, I [Doreen] lifted the shade and peeked out the window. Except for a sprinkle of stars and a sliver of a moon, it was now pitch-black outside. My sister's gentle snore let me know she was sound asleep. The TV was off and I had heard my parents' bedroom door close. It was time for my escape.

Earlier in the day I had picked out my best purse for this "runaway." It was red, rectangular in shape, with hinges on it, like a little suitcase, and a mirror on the lid. It could only hold my hairbrush, two pairs of panties, and a package of crackers. But for an eight-year-old, that was good enough. I was ready to go.

However, I began to have doubts. I considered how hard it would be to walk down the hall past my parents' bedroom without them hearing me because there was a board in the floor of the hallway that creaked. But if I attempted to open the heavy wooden window of our bedroom and tried to remove the screen, I knew for sure that my sister would wake up.

Suddenly, or so it seemed, those warm covers felt so good as I heard the wind blow through the trees on that chilly, late winter's eve. I couldn't seem to keep my eyes open. I fought it, but it felt like someone was gently closing them. The next thing I knew, it was morning, and once again, I had failed to make my great escape.

This scenario played out many times in my elementary years. But it wasn't until I was in my twenties, seeking help for challenges in my marriage, that I discovered why I continued to replay leaving home but never making my way out.

As a child, there were certain securities that kept me there. My mother loved me, food was always on the table, and I had a lovely home to live in. We lived in a middle-class neighborhood where I enjoyed many childhood friendships. I enjoyed spending time with both sets of grandparents who lived close by.

I remember the enjoyment of watching *Leave It to Beaver* and *Father Knows Best* on TV and wishing my dad was like one of those TV dads. From the age of five well into my teens, I loved watching the Miss America beauty pageants, and wished that I would someday be beautiful enough to be crowned a princess.

I wept deeply for the first time in my life as I spoke those words out loud to my counselor. He sat and listened as I began to describe occurrences that clearly displayed the lack of my father's acceptance throughout my life. This seemed to open the floodgates of memories and hurt and angry feelings I felt toward my father.

Seen but Not Heard

I recollected how resentful I was toward my dad for so often sending my sister and me to bed by six-thirty in the evening so he could have our mother to himself. Many summer nights I would peer out my bedroom window, yearning to be with the rest of the kids on the block who were playing hide-and-seek at dusk while I was supposed to be sleeping; all because my dad thought children were to be "seen and not heard." I believed that this was just a convenient out for him on many occasions, when those words followed his request that we leave the room.

I expressed to the counselor how I was told by my mother every night, for the first 12 years of my life, to "go and kiss your father good night," no matter how I felt. He most often sat comfortably in his easy chair, watching TV, expectant of my nightly kiss. I could not remember one time in my childhood when he came to tuck my sister or me into bed and kiss us goodnight. That longing was heightened when I saw my friends' dads do this for them whenever I had spent a night in their homes.

I recounted how, in my teen years, I dreaded our nightly family dinners. I would set the table thinking, *What will he find fault with tonight?* Would it be my acne? Or would I draw his criticism for putting butter on my bread? Or maybe it would be my posture, bringing a threat that he was going to make a wood brace that would force me to sit up straight.

His harsh, critical words about my appearance caused me to feel that I would never gain his favor or have boys interested in me.

I Will Prove Him Wrong

By this time I was becoming rebellious. I was determined to prove him wrong. I would get a boyfriend.

I found, in those early teen years, that flirting with the boys brought quick attention and some form of emotional gratification. I was so hungry for them to compliment me or just kiss me—validating me as a young woman. I didn't understand why all the other girls didn't flirt with the boys like I did. I thought it was fun. I lost the trust of some girlfriends and made enemies playing that game, luring the other girls' boyfriends away from them. But the relationships were short-lived so I thought, *What's the big deal?*

I looked for every opportunity to be away from home—a school football game, a party, a church activity, or anything else that was acceptable to my mother. My dad never minded how much time I spent away from home unless it interfered with the chores he required of me. In fact, I truly believed Dad appreciated my time away from home as much as I did.

By the age of 17, I was a senior in high school and had dated almost every guy I had hoped to. However, that had left me very lonely. I didn't even have a date to the senior prom. I had proved my father wrong, but all to no avail. I had isolated numerous potential girlfriends and was left with no boyfriend. I had a huge hole in my heart and nothing seemed to fill it.

The Man of My Dreams

Within two weeks of my high-school graduation, the man of my dreams came into my life. He had just finished a three-year term in the army and had returned home to establish himself in civilian life. He was the potential "catch" for every girl between the ages of 18 and 22 in the church where our families had attended for many years.

He was 22 years old and very handsome, over six feet tall, blue eyes, a great sense of humor, and—very important to a beach-city girl—a surfer! One night, as I jumped into the backseat of his parents' car for a ride home from church, there sat Chad. I was excited but jittery, knowing I was sitting right next to the "catch." I spoke more to his parents than to him because I was so nervous.

His dad pulled up in front of my house. As I slipped out of the car, Chad said, "Boy, those are some great legs!" My heart leaped—Chad Hanna thought I was pretty! By Friday he'd asked me out and within six months we were engaged.

At barely 19 years of age, marriage seemed like the best solution to escape my father's house. My dad viewed life with a strong work ethic. He did not regard higher education as a necessity and had informed me that if I were to consider going away to college, I'd have to pay for it myself. That seemed impossible. So I was soon working full-time and saving my money for a beautiful wedding.

My father was not happy that I was marrying Chad. I remember one day, just weeks before the wedding, he said to me, "I thought this would be a time in your life when you could spend some time with me." I couldn't believe my ears! I was instantly angry and thought, *He's ignored me for the last 19 years of my life and NOW he wants to spend time with me?* It was the first time in my life that I sensed I had begun to build a wall in my heart—a wall that I thought would keep my father from hurting me anymore.

The day of the wedding, as I stood waiting to go down the aisle on my father's arm, he turned and touched the edge of my veil. I thought for just a second that we were going to share a special moment. Instead he stated, "My mother would have never let this happen." I looked to see that my veil had been trimmed slightly unevenly. "Your grandmother would have trimmed this in satin," he stated proudly. Rightly so, my grandmother was a well-known seamstress and had I asked, I'm sure she would have done it for me. Once again, I had failed to meet my father's standards.

> *Life is pain, Highness.*
>
> *Anyone who says differently*
>
> *is selling something.*
>
> —THE PRINCESS BRIDE

Still, that walk down the aisle gave me such hope. I had proven that I could find a man to love me and would finally be free from my father. I believed that saying "I do" would eliminate my frustrated and angry feelings toward him. Yet, there I sat in a counselor's office 10 years later, dealing with all my "father" issues.

Break Down the Wall

With kindness and gentleness, my counselor helped me realize that the wall I had built in my heart ultimately never hurt my father; it only hurt me. He continued by saying that I would never be free emotionally or spiritually until I could forgive my father. *OFFER forgiveness?* I couldn't believe it. I thought to myself, *Shouldn't my dad be seeking MY forgiveness?*

As I left the counselor's office, pondering his advice to forgive my father, I drove to my parents' home to have a chat with my mother. I was considering the possibility that my memories might be distorted, and I wanted to gain her perspective.

As we sat and talked, things began to unfold. She told me something

I had never really understood before. I was a honeymoon baby. My father was not only shocked that, at 19 years of age, he was going to be a father within months of being married, he was also very disappointed that he was going to have the responsibilities of a father. He had told my mother prior to their wedding that he wasn't ready for children and had wanted to wait at least five years before starting a family.

So, upon my birth he found me an obstacle to having my mother fully to himself. Aha! Now I was beginning to understand why I had been sent to bed by six-thirty so many nights of my life!

My mom also told me how critical his mother and other members of my father's family had been toward him as a child, calling him various "pet names" that were very degrading. He, too, at the age of 18 couldn't wait to marry and flee from his home.

Driving home after chatting with my mom, I thought about what she had told me and seriously considered the words of my counselor. His desire was to free me from the inner turmoil that comes from harboring unforgiveness. In addition, he pointed out how this turmoil was overflowing into my marriage relationship—the reason I was there to see him originally! He explained to me that I had put many of my unfulfilled expectations of my father onto my husband. He then humorously expressed, "It would take at least three men to fulfill all that you are expecting your husband to fulfill!"

As I walked through the door of our home that night, I determined that I would seek Chad's forgiveness for the unrealistically high expectations I had placed upon him during our marriage. That night as we slipped into bed, I expressed to him how I now realized why I had been asking so much of him. I was trying to have him fulfill what I had desired from my father all of my life. He understood my feelings and forgave me.

I closed my eyes, at peace now with my husband, but still—what about my dad?

The Power of the Blessing

Within weeks after my counselor's challenge to forgive my father—which I wasn't yet ready to do—I went to a local bookstore to pick up a gift for a friend. While there, I happened to also pick up a book titled *The Gift of the Blessing*, authored by John Trent and Gary Smalley (Thomas Nelson, Inc., 1993). My eyes were immediately drawn to the following sentence on the cover:

> Dr. John Trent tells of his search to receive the blessing from his father and how, with the new insight he received from God through that search, he has sought to pick up the pieces of his shattered dream.

Those words jumped out at me. My dreams had been shattered and I was trying to pick up the pieces. And I surely did not want to be like my father. I wanted to do things differently for my daughters. I bought the book and began reading.

Chapter after chapter, I remember thinking, *Oh, how I wish my father had done that for me*. My self-pity was stopped short in the last chapter when Dr. Trent presented this challenge: "If you have not received your parents' blessing, begin to bless them and see what God will do." I was again confronted to face my "father" issues head-on.

Within days of finishing the book, I called my father and asked if I could take him to lunch—just the two of us. He said "yes" without hesitation, and we met together the next day. I can still remember exactly where we sat at a small Mexican restaurant in Cave Creek, Arizona.

As he finished his last few bites of an enchilada, I mustered up the courage to share my feelings. "Dad, I now know that when I was a child you demonstrated your love by providing a home for us, nice clothes, and food on the table. However, I've always felt that you didn't like me." Those were some of the hardest words I had ever spoken. I felt that by saying this out loud to my father, I was taking the risk of his complete rejection.

Conversely, he quickly responded, saying almost word for word what my mother had said about him: "I didn't want children immediately after marriage, and I was taught that children were to be seen and not heard." I could sense regret in his words, and it was reflected in his demeanor. For the first time in my life I felt sorry for my father, and the wall I had built in my heart began to crumble.

When he had finished talking, I said, "Dad, I want to have a good relationship with you; one that also includes my husband and children. With the counseling I have received recently, I've come to realize that I've had a deep resentment toward you for a long time. I would like for us to have a better relationship from here on, and I need to ask for your forgiveness. Will you forgive me?"

My father's eyes welled with tears as he replied, "Yes I will, and will you forgive me?"

I wept out those healing words: "Yes, Dad, I forgive you."

Wow! What a huge step in our relationship. While, in all honesty, I had hoped to hear "I love you," I was satisfied at that time with, "Will you forgive me?"

As the years progressed, our father/daughter relationship began to grow. We could laugh and talk together for the first time in our lives. From that day—he in his forties and I in my twenties—we were both seeking to grow spiritually, prompting engaging discussions between us.

In addition, at our now numerous family gatherings, I would delight as I watched my father and Chad enjoy each other's company.

The Perfect Father's Day Card

Some years later, I remember searching for several weeks, seeking to find the perfect Father's Day card. At the end of a discouraging search, I felt prompted to pray and ask the Lord if He had something that He wanted me to write for my father. As I lifted my head from prayer, it was as if suddenly the creative writer that was deep within me came out and my fingers began to speed across the keyboard, typing out a poem for my father.

I had never felt that I had a poetic gift until that day! I sat in amazement of my own work as I reread the poem. I quickly printed it out and sent it on its way to arrive by Father's Day.

My father and I were living several hundred miles apart at this time, so the following Sunday I called to wish him a happy Father's Day. I was so eager to find out whether he'd received the poem and hear his reaction to it that I urgently asked, "Dad, did you get my poem?"

He, rather casually, just said, "Yes, it was nice."

My heart dropped. I thought the poem was fabulous, and all I got was an "It was nice." I made every effort to mask my disappointment in his response. We went on to other topics of conversation. But as we were closing our phone call, he said, "I love you, Mija." Whenever my father called me *Mija* (a Spanish word of endearment), I always knew I was in his good graces. This was big—very big! I heard an "I love you" coupled with a "Mija!"

I quickly responded, "I love you, too, Dad." I got off the phone and fell into a heap of happy tears. I had heard the words I had yearned to hear all of my life from my father: "I love you."

Several months later, I had a business trip that took me to Phoenix,

Arizona, where my parents lived. When I arrived at m[
only my mother was there. We chatted for a few minu[
said, "Before your father gets here, I must show you something." She [
me into their bedroom, and there on the wall hung a two-by-three-foot
copy of the poem, done in calligraphy on parchment paper and lacquered
to a beautiful piece of wood. I wept with joy, not only realizing how much
he valued that gift, but also appreciating how often since that Father's
Day he had told me he loved me.

In that reflective moment, the thought came to me that I was living
out the last chapter of the *The Gift of the Blessing*, which stated, "If you
want to be a person who honors your parents, you will be a person who
blesses them. When you truly honor them and do what is right in God's
eyes, it will even prolong your life; living free of resentment and unforgiveness does prolong our lives, enabling us to live years longer!"[1]

Pam's Search

We sat across the table in a restaurant in Canada. My husband, Bill, and
I had just appeared on the TV show *Marriage Uncensored with Dave and
Christie*. Over dinner Dr. Dave Currie and his wife, Donalyn, along with
Bill and I, were talking about our children and our families of origin.
Dave and his wife have two remarkable daughters, whom we had met as
they sat in the studio audience that night.

As we sat at the table that evening, Dave shared a story that pen-
etrated me to the core. When his daughter Jody was a very little girl,
she came home and announced her love interest in a little boy. Dave
said to her, "Honey, when you are much older, there will be a day when
you will want to give your heart to a man. He will have to be really special, and you will need to feel confident that he is the one God wants

you to marry. Until then, I will keep your heart. I will keep it safe."

Dave's wife made a heart that hung in the Currie home and on it hung two gold keys, one for each daughter. Any time Dave prayed with his daughters, tucked them into bed, or acted out any of the other daily interactions a loving father would have with his daughter, he'd say, "And who has the key to your heart?" His daughters would answer, "You do, Daddy." Any time he had to set a rule or make a correction he would begin with, "Remember who has the key to your heart?" And the girls would answer, "You do, Daddy."

Then Dave would explain how because he, their daddy, had their best interests at heart, he had to make decisions and choices to protect his daughters and provide the very best path for them. Dave would explain, "God has called me to do this because God and Daddy love both of you little girls very much."

Dave shared, "One day Jody met and fell in love with a fabulous man, Chris. She came to me and asked if she could have her heart now because she had found the man she wanted to give it to. I agreed and prayed and released her heart."

The day of their wedding, Dave asked one last time, "Who has the key to your heart?" But this time the answer was different; it was the name of her new husband.

Then Dave sang a song he had written for this moment, "The Transfer of the Sacred Trust":

As man to man, we stand here today,
Though the time is so right, I won't give her away.
Yet you are my answer to the prayer for God's plan
Please listen close, Son, as I give you her hand.

God gave me a trust as head of my home
To look after my family, to protect through life's storm,
To comfort and build these put in my care
And cover them daily with a fatherly prayer . . . that's why

I won't let her go, but I will let you start.
To treasure her most, you must carry her heart.
I'll still be her dad, but relinquish I must,
It's the transfer of the sacred trust,
The transfer of the sacred trust.

There comes a day in every girl's life
About leaving and cleaving, 'bout becoming a wife,
I've protected her heart from all other men
The depth of this moment, please understand.

God gives you this trust now as head of your home
To look after my daughter, to protect through life's storm,
Your love dare not waver as you carry her heart
Please hold her real close as I did from the start . . . you see

I won't let her go, but I will let you start.
To treasure her most, you carry her heart.
I'll still be her dad, but relinquish I must,
It's the transfer of the sacred trust,
It's the transfer of the sacred trust,
I transfer now my sacred trust.[2]
(reprinted with permission)

Right after he sang the song, he gave Chris, his new son-in-law, the key that had hung in the Currie home, the key to his daughter's heart. Then six years later, for his second daughter, Keldy, Dave repeated the passing of this sacred trust, and gave the key to her heart to her new husband, also a prince of a man.

A dedicated dad holds the key to the heart of his Modern-Day Princess until the day God's prince of a husband comes to care for the heart of that precious young woman. It is a sacred trust, passing from the two men who should love a woman more than any other: a father, then a husband.

I sat at the table weeping because that is the kind of love I had always longed for as a daughter. That is the kind of love that builds courage and confidence into a young woman's heart and life.

Looking for My Key

In a nutshell, I grew up in a home that was confusing. One night I might be dancing around the living room with my daddy, but the next night he might be in a drunken rage banishing me to my bedroom in fear. I would slide my chest of drawers in front of the door to keep him from coming in my room while he was so angry. I always thought our family might make the front-page news, but not for a good reason, rather a headline that would read, "Man shoots family then shoots himself."

When I was in high school, one night I was awakened from a deep sleep to my mother screaming, "Help me!" We three kids bolted from our beds, running through a pitch-black house thinking, *Oh no! We need to rescue Mom!* We broke open the door into the garage and there we found, not my mom in need of rescue, but rather my daddy, trying to hang himself from the rafters of the garage.

My brother, Bret, a high-school football player, pulled my dad down and dragged him into the living room, pushing him onto the sofa. I took the noose off his neck and began to pray aloud over my father. I knelt and prayed with my siblings and my mother for hours, singing hymns, praying, and begging God to rescue my father from himself.

Abba, Father

Later that same day, God spoke to my heart, "Pam, you have been pushing Me away. You must think I am like your earthly father: distant, demanding, and demeaning. I am not like that! Open up the Bible; find out who I am." Shortly after that day, I came upon Romans 8:15, which says we call God "Abba, Father." I was reminded again of the reason I made the decision to begin a relationship with Him. I recalled in a powerful way that the King of Kings was my Daddy and He loved me unconditionally. My best interests were and are on His heart. It was as if He were saying, "Who has the key to your heart?" *You do, Daddy, my Abba Father. I am Your daughter, a daughter of the King.*

> *I think the biggest disease the world suffers from in this day and age is the disease of people feeling unloved.*
>
> —DIANA, PRINCESS OF WALES

For the next three years I kept a journal, and I wrote down all the verses I found that showed God loved me and was a Father I could trust. That journey was my personal rite of passage into becoming a woman of God. Those verses placed my tiara on my head as I was crowned a Modern-Day Princess. Because of this journey, I was able to recognize my own prince, Bill, when God sent him into my life. I could see that Bill, a healthy, godly man who loved me fully, was worthy to hold the key to my heart.

God sent many people into my life to help me understand what it meant to be God's princess. You will hear some of those stories, and hear more of my own journey to grasp what it means to be a daughter of the King.

Highly Motivated, Greatly Needed

You see, the two of us [Pam and Doreen] are highly motivated to help young women learn what it means to be daughters of the King. Somehow girls around the world have lost their way. Consider the following statistics:

One in three girls becomes pregnant before age 20.[3] The median age at which young women have their first sexual experience is 17.[4] One in four will contract an STD (sexually transmitted disease).[5] Forty percent of girls at a contraceptive clinic are there without their parents' knowledge.[6] One-third of all teen pregnancies will end in an abortion.[7]

We also know that many girls are turning into bullies. Nearly one-third of all juvenile arrests are girls, and one-third of all property crimes are perpetrated by girls. About one-quarter of all aggravated assaults are committed by girls.[8] A girl is more likely to be violent at home, and the victim more than any other is her mother.[9]

Dr. Dallas Jackson, professor of educational leadership at Argosy University/Tampa and assistant principal of curriculum at Morgan Fitzgerald Middle School in Pinellas County, Florida, says, "Over 50 percent of the bullying incidences involve one girl picking on another."[10] Cyber bullying has made picking on each other more common and deadly.

On March 30, 2008, high-school cheerleader Victoria Lindsay was lured to a friend's home in Lakeland, Florida. While two boys stood guard outside the house, six girls attacked Lindsay. They knocked her unconscious by slamming her head against a wall. Then the perpetrators posted the attack on the Internet. After the authorities arrested the teens involved, one asked if she would "make cheer practice," apparently uncaring of the seriousness of the attack.[11]

Cyber bullying can consist of mean or critical comments, sharing personal information in a public setting, or demeaning or undermining another girl's social standing. Today, this kind of pain can travel at light speed through text messaging, IM chatting, or social-networking postings.

And girls pick on the guys, too. On December 5, 2004, the *Ottawa Citizen* reported: "Considerably more boys than girls say their dates yell at them, demean them, pinch them, slap them, and out-and-out attack them, according to preliminary findings in a study on dating violence."[12]

However, teen girls are hardest on themselves. Teenage girls are more likely to develop depression than teenage boys.[13] (The Heritage Foundation found that those who were sexually active had a much higher depression rate.) Depression in girls might also extend to behaviors like cutting, anorexia, bulimia, and other self-destructive behaviors. Girls experiment with drugs and alcohol in higher numbers than boys.[14] Often, girls use drugs and alcohol to lose weight.[15]

"Girls think about and attempt suicide about twice as often as boys, and tend to attempt suicide by overdosing on drugs or cutting themselves."[16] A new, desperate, self-destructive behavior is "sexting," which includes text messaging pornographic photos of themselves; over 20 percent of girls have engaged in this risky behavior.[17]

Consider the young women around you. Can you think of just one girl you know who seems to have lost her way? When I [Pam] met Emily, she was suffering from the hurt and pain of a dysfunctional family. Her mother, distracted by her own pain, was unable to help her daughter. Emily needed someone to care enough to come alongside her, to reach out and show her God's love. There are Emilys all around us.

My [Pam's] motivation in writing this book was heightened on September 5, 2007, the day my first granddaughter, Eden, was born. Even while she was in utero, and since, I have prayed she will step into her priceless identity as a daughter of the King. I pray that her mother, Hannah, will have all she needs to impart a godly heritage to her. I know my son Brock will impart a blessing on his daughter because he already does, in the way he gently loves and cares for Eden. But I also know Eden will need more voices, more wisdom—the help of mentors—to help her safely step into, and then walk out, her identity in Christ.

Can you hear a host of teen girls crying, asking, and waiting for your help and guidance? Right now, think of a young woman, a tween or teen, you might know. She may be your daughter, your niece, or just a young girl you're acquainted with. You could be the person in her life to dust off her tiara, place it on her head, and help her see herself as God sees her—a person valued and loved. And you could do this for *many* girls, moving a multitude of young women into a healthy, whole, and wholesome future as adult women who make a difference for their generation.

Out there among you, there are many "Doreens" who are longing for affirmation; "Pams" who are longing for attention; "Emilys" who are longing for affection; and "Edens" who are looking for agreement. One voice to confirm her value can make all the difference in a girl's life. Every girl deserves a mentor, a mom, and a memorable blessing—a rite of passage to womanhood—and a chance to be a woman who reflects God's character and lives it out to leave a positive imprint in a world that so desperately needs it.

Mentor Moment

It's Mother's Day, and I [Pam] answer my cell phone often. I have only three sons, but several young women will call me on this special day and thank me for being their "spiritual mom." Though I am not a biological mom of daughters, I am a mentor to many women.

Let me share my journey to becoming a mentor. It first began when a series of women sacrificed their time and energy to mentor me. I, myself, had a terrific mom who came to know Christ the same year that I did. I was 8, my mom, 28. But I grew up in a home filled with the drama of an alcoholic father prone to domestic violence. My first mentors were two women I didn't even know were mentors until years later because I had no idea what the word *mentor* even meant! They were two of my mother's friends, Kathy and Mrs. Beamer.

Both of these special women saw the chaos in our family and compassionately invited us to attend church with them. At Kathy's home, I saw what a healthy marriage looked like and how a healthy family functioned. At Sunday school, Mrs. Beamer taught me about Jesus, the Author of love, and prepared my heart for the personal decision to receive Jesus that I would make before my ninth birthday.

What I learned most from these women was:

- Love lavishly and trust the results to God.
- Be faithful in the little things because you don't know how that little act of kindness, integrity, or wisdom might ripple to impact hundreds, thousands, even millions of people.

In college, I was looking for love in all the wrong places, trying to add up awards and accolades in a frantic search for self-worth that was leaving me feeling empty. As I watched my parents' marriage implode and fall apart, I felt helpless and very alone in life. I was a young woman with a heart to do good but a fatal flaw inside my heart threatened to destroy my life before it ever really got started.

At the time, I had an overstated need for male attention. I was a virgin at 18 but a tease and very disjointed in my personal value system. I just wasn't sure what I believed about much of anything. It was as if I had been dropped by a plane into a vast wilderness, and I was looking for my compass. In my life, Tina, my next mentor, became the compass giver.

I met Tina at a Campus Crusade Bible study; she was the woman who, with her husband, organized the event. Tina asked me questions, hard ones at times: Who did I think Jesus was? What did I think my life purpose was? Did I read the Bible? Attend church? Tina also answered my questions, held me accountable to make wise choices, expected me to reach higher and further in my goals, and challenged me to be a better person and leader than I had ever pictured for my life. She encouraged me to dress more modestly, act more lady-like, think more critically about principles, and decide more strategically about my future and my place in the world.

Her nurturing of me in the area of what constitutes healthy dating, engagement, and marriage set the foundation for the strong, vibrant marriage I have today. I would have completely missed my godly, amazing husband, Bill, had Tina not entered my world and gotten me unaddicted to men. She pushed me to interview couples with healthy marriages to get a better view of which dating boundaries work best. She pointed me to God and Scripture to form my core relationship values.

What I learned from Tina:

- Always ask the tough questions.
- Expect the best from people, and they will rise to meet those expectations.
- Be a woman of sure principles in an unsure world.

The woman who mentored Tina also mentored me. Her name is Faith. Faith and her husband, Cal, had a vision for building a home across the street from the college campus where students could come and find wisdom, training, and a safe place to make better choices in life as they were launching out on their own.

I came to Faith because I was in a dilemma: I had overcommitted myself with extracurricular activities. Faith listened to my heart, prayed with me, gave me some Scripture verses to read, and then said something like, "Pam, you have a pure heart for God. I am sure God will lead you through His Word to the answer you need." And God did. As I read one of the verses about not "loving the world," I realized my future was in serving Jesus. I was to invest in that path for my future. It was a clear call.

What I learned from Faith:

- Love the Lord and love His Word, and you'll have all the answers you need.

- Treat young people with respect, and trust that if you give them the tools, God will lead them.
- Relationships matter. God uses relationships to expand His work.

This last one has an important side-note story. Faith mentored me, but she also had similar meetings with a young college woman named Mary. That same Mary ended up going on staff with Campus Crusade, then was hired to be president of Women of Faith.

It was while Doreen was working for Women of Faith that she and I met. Doreen was in Kansas laying the groundwork for Women of Faith. I was speaking at an event in Kansas where she gave an announcement for the upcoming Women of Faith event. I was speaking on *Women of Influence* and gave a message on mentoring! Now, years later, all those connections (and more) led us to write this book on raising and mentoring young women.

In seminary and ministry, I have had a series of women invest in my life. When I look back on these women, and others who poured their time, talent, and trust into my life, I realize God was preparing me for living an adventure with Him.

What Is a Rite of Passage?

God put the Man into a deep sleep. As he slept he removed one
of his ribs and replaced it with flesh. God then used the rib
that he had taken from the Man to make Woman.

—Genesis 2:21 (MSG)

If I could write a prescription for the women of this world,
I would provide each of them with a healthy dose of self-esteem
and personal worth (taken three times a day until the symptoms
disappear). I have no doubt this is their greatest need.[1]

—Dr. James Dobson

Ritz package? Is that what you said?" asked a cute, quizzical, and hungry teenager. I [Doreen] was attempting to explain a rite of passage to a group of teenage girls. She, like many other teen girls and their parents, had no clue what a rite of passage was because it has not been a widely celebrated event in our modern-day, American culture. To help you grasp the importance of a rite of passage in the life of a young lady, we want to first share various different rites of passage that are the norm in other cultures.

In the Jewish Community

A Jewish girl's rite of passage is called a bat mitzvah. At the age of 12 she is paired with a woman mentor, someone other than her mother, who will come alongside her for one year to train her in all the ways of Jewish womanhood, solidifying all that she has been taught by her parents and religious community.

In preparation for her bat mitzvah, she memorizes a passage from the Torah (the first five books of the Bible). She also receives further instruction about her family's religion and their culture. Her mentor helps her to strengthen her talents and gifts and define her future career goals. The young girl also learns appropriate etiquette and receives instruction in the importance of giving to the poor. Most often she is required to volunteer on a weekly basis during that year in a shelter, hospital, or charity organization of her choice.

On her 13th birthday, with family, friends, and those within her synagogue, she celebrates her rite of passage. In preparation for the celebration, she and her mother go shopping for a dress that is equivalent to a wedding dress. Then on the special day she stands in her synagogue before all who were invited and reveals her knowledge of the Torah by quoting a portion from memory. She demonstrates her talent, expresses her future goals, and states where she will share 10 percent of her gifts with the poor. The climactic moment comes when her rabbi and father publicly bless her.

Once a young girl completes her bat mitzvah, she has the responsibilities of an adult under Jewish law. She is not considered "innocent" anymore, and is responsible for her own actions. Traditionally, the parents of the young girl give thanks to God that they no longer have to carry the burden of their child's sins. The dinner after the ceremony is usually quite elaborate as many family and friends are invited to this celebration and many attending bring very generous gifts.[2]

In Latin America

Latinos in North and South America alike are well acquainted with the financial burdens of throwing what is known in their culture as a "Quinceañera" or a "Fiesta de los quince." This celebration typically occurs on or near a young girl's 15th birthday, hence the name (*quince* [pronounced keen-say] means 15 in Spanish). Some parents take additional part-time jobs, go into debt, or save for years to pay for a celebration that can cost more than fifteen thousand dollars (perhaps an even better reason for the name). The ceremony reflects the coming-of-age celebrations rooted in the traditions of Spain and indigenous cultures of Latin America.

Quinceañera ceremonies are held most often within the Catholic Church for the purpose of seeking the church's and God's blessings. Following the ceremony in some South American countries is the celebration that includes the giving and throwing of a *quince* doll, signifying the young lady's last doll as a child. The young lady throws the doll to the other female children in attendance, similar to the tradition of the bride throwing the bouquet at a wedding reception.

The celebrant wears "flats," or flat shoes, for the celebration. But, after the inaugural dance, the father of the young lady seats her on a chair in the center of the dance floor, removes her flats (girl shoes), and places high heels on her feet, signifying that she has become a young lady. Then she dances her first dance with her father.

At most parties, the girl wears a pink dress (a symbol of her femininity) and a tiara. She presides over a court of 14 girls (*damas*) and 15 boys (*chambelanes*), which, including herself, equals 30 people, or 15 couples (one to represent each year of her life). At the party, her court dances a waltz and one surprise dance. In earlier times, the party indicated that a girl was ready for marriage. In today's culture it signifies that she can date.[3]

In the Navajo Nation

When a Navajo girl reaches puberty there is a special five-day ritual called a Kinaalda. This ceremony, with ancient roots, invites the "Spirit of Changing Woman" into the girl's life. She has learned from her own mother and other women from her tribe about the personal qualities and practices that will help her succeed as a Navajo wife and mother.

The Kinaalda takes place in a hogan (hut), built to house all who will attend. In preparation for the Kinaalda, the young Navajo girl receives instruction from a woman selected to mold and train her. She learns, hands-on, about her Navajo heritage and how she will be expected to take care of herself, her family, and her people. She also receives instruction from the Hataalii (the medicine man), who oversees all the tribe's rituals and leads the spiritual ceremony concluding the Kinaalda.

The pressure on the young girl is enormous, and her behavior is con-sidered critical to the success of her Kinaalda. She must cheerfully and gracefully serve, with no complaints or show of bad temper. She must also greet, serve, clean, and cook for all who attend. She must prepare a special corn cake to serve to her guests, although she will not partake of it. The corn cake is accompanied by many other goods and gifts to be given to the guests to demonstrate one of the qualities most important to Navajos—generosity.

Throughout her time of training, she also runs three times a day to prepare for her most important run, which happens early in the morning of the day of her celebration, after an all-night sing. The purpose of the practice runs is to build endurance and develop judgment, each run going farther and at a faster pace. On her final morning run she must run from the hogan along a designated path and return before dawn, prior to the Hataalii's last song. This concludes her Kinaalda, validating her now as a young Navajo woman.[4]

In the American Culture

While formal rites of passage have rarely been celebrated in our American culture, they are now beginning to increase in number, type, and popularity for boys and girls. The following section outlines various types of rites of passage for young girls in American society today.

The Debutante Ball

This has been the most familiar rite of passage for American teenage girls. These events are still held today by various charity organizations and are most often held for upper-class families. This normally requires the father to be a member of the sponsoring organization. The young girls, from the ages of 13 to 16, receive instruction in beauty enhancement, etiquette, dance, and community service. The debutante's night of celebration brings with it the excitement of wearing her first formal dress and practicing her newly acquired etiquette. It culminates in the highlight of the evening: her first dance with her father.

The Purity Ball

The purity ball is normally held in a hotel and is open to the community for dads and daughters to attend. It can be held in various settings for churches, groups, or families who want to celebrate their daughters' commitment to purity. The Father/Daughter Purity Ball is a memorable ceremony for fathers to sign commitments to be responsible men of integrity. The commitment also includes their vow to protect their daughters in their choices for purity. The daughters silently commit to live pure lives before God through the symbol of laying down a white rose at the cross.

Helena, age 11, attended a Father/Daughter Purity Ball in Albuquerque, New Mexico, in November of 2008 with her father, Joe. This is her story:

> During the summer, even before I knew I was going to a Purity Ball, my mom and I walked by an antique shop. We decided to have some fun and go inside. I saw a beautiful vintage-style peach dress and told my mom that I loved it. A few weeks before the Ball, my mom surprised me—she had bought the dress. My mom was as excited as I was.
>
> You have to be at least 11 years old to attend the Purity Ball and I turned 11 on November 11, three days before the Ball.
>
> Getting ready for the Ball was almost as much fun as the evening itself. I took a long, hot bubble bath, we did my nails, curled my hair, and Mom even let me wear a bit of makeup. I could tell the evening was going to be a wonderful time in my life.
>
> One of the first things I remember about the night of the Ball was my dad telling me I looked gorgeous; that made me feel really special and having my dad take me that night made me respect him in a bigger way.
>
> Before we danced, there were teachers who talked about the difference between beauty on the inside and being "hot." Hot is

being very pretty on the outside, but there is nothing on the inside that makes you beautiful. They said that what makes a girl beautiful is what is inside, in her heart. They talked about making a commitment to be pure until we were married.

One thing I saw while listening to their talks was a dad and daughter sitting in front of us. Each time there was something good said, the father would hug and whisper encouragement to his daughter; that made me feel happy for them.

I loved dancing with my dad; we did lots of our favorite silly dances and we laughed a lot together.

That night too, my dad gave me a purity ring. I made a commitment to my father to stay pure until I get married. I have not taken my ring off since. I feel more confident now after the Purity Ball to be committed to staying pure. I feel I can talk more openly with my parents today and I have noticed, too, that my dad tells me more often nice things about me.

I am already looking forward to doing this again someday.

For more information about purity balls, go to http://generations oflight.myicontrol.com/.

The "Becoming a Modern-Day Princess" Program

The *Becoming a Modern-Day Princess* curriculum can be implemented through the next three styles of rites of passage (family, church, and community). The girl can go through the *Becoming a Modern-Day Princess Journal* with her mother or with a group of friends. These Modern-Day Princess groups can be sponsored by a church, a community group, or friends and families. Over a period of seven or more weeks, girls participate in relevant discussions and fun and interesting character-building activities, in order to help them understand and appreciate their transition to womanhood. We'll take a closer look at this specific rite of passage in chapter 4.

A Family Celebration

The family-based rite of passage represents a more intimate process, where the core family is well established and has the opportunity and resources to provide their daughter with a more personally focused blessing ceremony. An age for this passage is established by the parents, setting precedence for the siblings who will follow. Some families have these celebrations at a certain-age birthday, as a teen enters high school or begins to date, before her senior year, or at graduation. This time-honored passage will create anticipation rather than fear of the transition into adulthood; and the children will view it as a family tradition.

Depending on the parents' choice, a mother may take her daughter through a journey of preparation, or she may choose a mentor to be her daughter's guide. This journey can take a weekend, several weeks, or up to one year. Some families also choose this type of rite of passage to confirm a young girl's commitment to sexual purity by giving her a purity ring or some other special gift of significance.

> *The best and most beautiful things in the world cannot be seen, nor touched . . . but are felt in the heart.*
>
> —HELEN KELLER

In preparation for her celebration, her parents formally invite family and friends to attend the ceremony. Normally, the family's pastor, priest, or other spiritual leader attends for the purpose of imparting his blessing upon the event, the family, and the girl. Various mentors and family mem-

bers offer an abundance of blessings and prayers as well. The pinnacle is
the father's blessing. Then, all in attendance are challenged to come alongside the girl to support her in this journey to womanhood. Food, fellowship, and the giving of a piece of jewelry or family heirloom might be
included; sometimes a special dance with her father highlights the closing of the event.

Here is a letter that carries the sentiment of the value that a rite of passage family celebration can provide:

Dear Doreen,

*We had Madison's Princess Ball/Blessing Ceremony last Sunday
night and it was magical. We used the* DOK *curriculum and read
Angela Thomas's book* Do You Think I'm Beautiful *as preparation
for her night.*

*The weekend was fabulous. It started on Friday night as my
husband took our daughter out for dinner and presented her with
a beautiful purity ring. Then, on Sunday evening we invited 90
guests to join us at a restaurant down on Lake Erie, where we had
decorated with pink and white tulle wrapped in twinkle lights,
beautiful flowers, and candles on the tables.*

*The evening started with a time of fellowship and food, with
punch served in tall plastic champagne flutes. When the ceremony
began, everyone was seated at tables surrounding the dance floor
and we had our 15-year-old son escort his sister to her mom and
dad as the song "Amazing Love" played in the background. Our
pastor had everyone stand and welcome her as they sang the chorus
"You Are My King, Jesus, You Are My King."*

*We had created a video that told her life story from the day she
was born right up till just weeks before her party. We wanted to set*

the stage about how much God loves and cherishes her. Our pastor then spoke about why we were having this rite-of-passage/blessing ceremony and the importance of it.

I had invited four women who are mentors in Madison's life. They each came forward and spoke words of blessing and wisdom into her life. Then, we laid hands on her and prayed for her. Madison spoke about what she had learned in our study together. Then her daddy got up and spoke words of blessing into her life.

At that point, he asked my mother to join us. She handed him Madison's tiara and then he blessed her by putting it onto her head. Then I read a poem I had written to Madison about the dance she was about to partake in, an earthly representation of a spiritual picture that God had given us about dancing.

God wants Madison and, I believe, each one of us, to know how much He desires to dance that dance of life with us. Not just one or two dances but our whole life, close in His arms, secure in knowing that He knows every step and that He will keep us close to him no matter what.

So out onto the dance floor my husband, Gary, went. I read the poem to Madison, and the song "Unnamed Hymn," by Chris Rice played. Gary extended his hand inviting his daughter to choose to come out onto that dance floor and say "yes" to him and to God, acknowledging that she desires to spend the rest of her life dancing in the arms of her Heavenly Father.

This signaled the beginning of the rest of her life and for the party to start. People stayed and danced and fellowshipped until after 1:00 A.M. It blew me away. The whole evening was the exact picture the Lord had given to me two years ago and had turned out 10 times better than I could have even desired.

The Lord was glorified. Madison was built up, encouraged, blessed, and ready to move into this next season of life, sure of who she is and where she is heading. Many people who attended shared stories of how touched they were and how it had challenged them to do this for their own children, or how it had prompted them to make changes in their own relationships with their grown children.

—Joyfully submitted by Julie Hayes

This family sacrificed much to create a memorable evening for their daughter, but the price tag might be beyond what you are able to handle and that is completely fine. Sometimes a smaller budget forces our minds to be more creative so do not be discouraged by limited funds—God will meet you with His ingenuity as you pray for wisdom on how to make the marking of this moment special.

Rites of passage can be just as meaningful with a more modest budget. It isn't the place that matters as much as what you communicate to your daughter in that place. Some ideas might include a tea at your home where the women of the family gather and bless the teen. It could be a mother/daughter overnight adventure in a nice hotel—or at a lakeside campground. You'll find many more tips and ideas throughout this book for hosting an economical rite of passage for your daughter.

A Church-Based Program

The church-based rite of passage has grown in popularity in the United States because of the availability of resources, mentors (older women within the church who have a heart for teenage girls, or women youth leaders), and men of integrity who can impart a blessing when fathers are not present.

Churches are completely free to emphasize the spiritual component of a teen girl's life in a biblically based rite of passage. Churches also provide an already established group of girls of appropriate ages. A rite-of-passage program offers a healthy environment promoting a spirit of camaraderie, which can nurture lifelong friendships.

The church, most often, can help provide the resources for a lovely celebration held there with a staff pastor presiding over the ceremony. Many recommendations made under the community-based rite-of-passage section also apply to church-group rites of passage.

One of the greatest joys of participating in a biblically based rite of passage is seeing Malachi 4:6 being revealed before your very eyes: "He will turn the hearts of the fathers to their children, and the hearts of the children to their fathers. . . ."

You might be a church leader who picked up this book because you want to carry out a rite of passage for the young women of your church. However, you might also be a volunteer or parent who recognizes that the youth pastor, pastoral staff, and director of women's ministry are very busy people; God could be asking you to step up and be a parent coordinator or volunteer coordinator for a rite-of-passage event.

A rite-of-passage journey and celebration are usually easy to recruit help for because often many parents are very excited to team together to create a memorable evening for their daughters. By teaming up and pooling the time, talent, and financial resources of the local church, youth group, and the families of the participants, a very lovely, life-changing event can be created.

In this case, the responsibility of the event is spread over many people so no one feels overly stressed or financially pressed. The synergy of a team can add to the camaraderie the girls are developing as they meet for their rite-of-passage study. Often the adults are positively affected by observing a rite-of-passage ceremony, as is exhibited in this letter about a church-sponsored event:

Dear Doreen,

I want to share the wonderful results of our rite-of-passage celebration. I had asked you to pray for my daughter and those girls who I knew would have the challenge of not being sure their fathers would impart blessings to them. I did not believe that the blessing would be the same if not imparted by their father and, I admit, I was afraid it would break my daughter's heart.

The Wednesday before our Saturday celebration, my daughter, Katie, found out that her father would not be imparting a blessing to her. He had told her all along that he would, and she was just so hurt and could not believe he would not do this one thing for her.

We asked Les, a deacon from our church, to accept the role of father representative to Katie, even though he did not really know her that well. Les was nervous and Katie was not sure what to expect, but I want you to know that this was totally orchestrated by GOD! I will tell you that my faith was tested because I was really hoping for a wonderful night for Katie.

Les brought her flowers and a little stuffed puppy dog. He laminated the verse he chose for her and put the date on the back and everything! When she stood up there, he said wonderful things about her. She cried, he cried, we all cried. I am so very proud of her for going through the program despite her father issues.

What a wonderful thing God did. Les had never been able to pass his Christian faith to his daughters, now grown, and for him it was as if God was giving him this second chance to do the right thing. Les actually apologized to Katie that, because of the choices we divorced parents make, we have made life harder on our kids. Katie told me she felt like a million dollars! Les has continued to build his relationship with Katie by talking to her and letting her know that he is available for her anytime.

Close friends of mine were touched by the whole celebration, most of us with "father issues." We realized how our lives and the decisions we have made would have been different if we had had a program like this. How many hurts could have been healed and how much stronger as women we could have been.

So many of the girls in our group had strained relationships with their fathers and some were not sure their dads would come through; even strong Christian men were getting cold feet. I want you to know that every girl who stood on that stage cried. For some of them it was the first time their dads had said they were proud of them or that they loved them.

As for the dads, each of them had to stop and compose himself because he was filled with such emotion. One father confessed and asked for his daughter's forgiveness for not being the father he should have been. Another dad thanked his daughter for bringing him back to church. GOD is so awesome!

Katie and the others will forever be changed because of their participation in their DOK rite of passage and celebration. May God continue to lead you and bless your every step.
—Vicki V.

Christian camps and conference centers are also possible opportunities for a church-based rite-of-passage event. They can offer girls the opportunity to go through a curriculum or program over the course of a week or weekend. The families are invited to the camp at the end of the week or weekend, Dad brings his prepared blessing to the camp, and the celebration happens there with many families participating together in a beautiful atmosphere supplied by the conference center.

A Community-Based Program

A community-based rite of passage can encompass a number of girls from a related community group, such as members of local youth organizations, Girl Scout; Boys & Girls Clubs, Youth for Christ groups, or private schools; or it can be as simple as a group of girls within a local neighborhood. It usually works best when groups are no larger than 10 or 12 for the purpose of building intimacy among the girls and the potential growth of healthy friendships.

The benefit of incorporating the Becoming a Modern-Day Princess Community-Based Rite of Passage within an existing curriculum or an after-school program is that this material is specifically designed for a nonreligious setting but still communicates lasting values and healthy advice to teen girls. It can be adapted into whatever setting, location, or group that already exists for young women.

Because the community-based passage can involve "at risk" teen girls, some may be concerned about the lack of a father or man who will impart her public affirmation. Father representatives can range from various family members (grandfathers, uncles, cousins) to other respected men in their lives

> *Deeply embedded in the heart of every Christian parent there is a longing desire that their children will embrace their faith and values.*
>
> —JOHN FICHTNER

(group-home representatives, athletic-program coaches, teachers, pastors, close friends). Or, the rite-of-passage facilitator can seek a group blessing by a man whom the girls all respect.

For those who are interested in coordinating a community-based rite of passage for a group of girls, the celebration can be held in a home, local activity center, church, or wherever seating is available for family and friends to attend. You may wish to keep costs at a minimum because many less fortunate families do not have the financial resources to provide a formal dress, expensive jewelry, or an elaborate celebration. Even so, the celebration can be just as grand with the help of others.

Seek help within your local community whenever possible. Many vendors, leaders, churches, and non-profit organizations as well as business owners may be willing to donate to such a worthy cause. Remember that local stores are often looking for opportunities to serve their community, especially for life-impacting events for children and teens. A list of ideas of "Items to Ask For" is in the back of this book, as well as some worksheets to help with planning and executing your event.

Below is a letter regarding a community-based rite of passage:

Dear Doreen,

On May 27 we concluded our rite-of-passage journey with our celebration. Because we desired to not ask anything monetarily from these un-churched parents, we asked various local stores for contributions. They enabled us to have a beautiful decorated hall and wonderful refreshments, and the flowers for the girls were donated by a florist.

God keeps blowing me away with what He can do in the lives of people. The girls did great! The men—boy, did they step up to the plate with the job they did! Nine girls, four dads, five stand-in-the-gap men—it was powerful.

Let me tell you about Erin P. She had just recognized the one-year anniversary of her father's death in a tragic motorcycle accident the weekend before the ceremony. Yet, she did so well when it was her time to share. She said that God had revealed to her when we studied "Men of Integrity" that God wanted her to be able to open her heart up to other men He was placing in her life to love and guide her now that her father is gone.

She was struggling so much with that issue before starting the rite of passage because she thought it would mean she didn't love her dad anymore or that someone else was going to replace him. Praise God that she now sees the truth and was actually able to communicate that to everyone in her speech that night. She had her grandfather bless and dance with her. It was beautiful!

His Princess,

Julie H.

Youth for Christ/Youth Unlimited Community Outreach

Elgin County, Ontario, Canada

Common Characteristics of Rites of Passage

As I [Doreen] researched these various rites of passage, I found a number of similarities. Following is a list you might find interesting and helpful in understanding the need for celebrating our girls' transition into womanhood.[5]

- Rites of passage celebrate the transition from adolescence to adulthood (age of initiating a celebration differs by culture but ranges between the ages of 11 and 16).
- The older women (mothers and mentors) teach the younger women.
- Most often the preparation prior to a celebration addresses the key elements of a girl's whole person—body, soul, and spirit.
- Character qualities are always held in high esteem.
- Spiritual beliefs are a foundation in almost all ceremonies.
- A girl's father or another respected man in her life seals her rite of passage through his blessing.
- Family and friends participate in the celebration.

While many cultures offer some kind of a rite of passage, many families, many daughters, still have no moment planned that celebrates this vital transition in a young woman's life. What about the young woman in your life? Or the young women in your sphere of influence? Who will create this special moment for them? Would a family event be best, or would you like to work within a friendship circle or organization your daughter and her friends are already a part of?

For all forms of the rite of passage, I [Doreen] recommend implementation of the passage and celebration at the age of 13 or 14 because this is normally the age range of girls transitioning out of elementary school into junior high or middle school and when they are reaching puberty. However, many girls between the ages of 15 and 18, high-school age, who have not had this opportunity at an earlier age, excitedly seek to participate and should be embraced or have a separate high-school group created for them.

If the group ends up as a mixed-age group, the older girls usually serve as excellent role models for the younger. One important recommendation: If the group combines junior-high and high-school girls, it is wise to separate the two age groups (12–14 and 15–18) during group discussion because of the maturity level of discussion, especially when sisters participate together.

Your choice to adopt this recommendation is dependent upon the facilitators and mentors for each particular group. If it is an age-diverse group and two discussion groups are needed, then two mentors who work as a team are a nice leadership combination.

Perhaps you are a leader in a youth organization or church and you can become a point person to gather many families together and create a tradition in your congregation. Begin praying for that young woman or those young women who motivated your heart to pick up this book. God has a plan for her (or them) and you are a part of that plan in some way. Close your eyes, and picture that special young lady with a crown on her head, a smile on her face, and her father's blessing ringing in her ears and treasured in her heart. Her life, and yours, will never be the same—they will be so much better!

Laying the Groundwork—Starting Traditions

A rite of passage is a family tradition worthy of implementing generation after generation. Traditions are the tools that God uses to knit a cord of truth and love from generation to generation. There is power in a tradition. For example, our [Pam's] family has become known as the "family of many traditions." We believe traditions are living word pictures that pass on the most precious beliefs from generation to generation.

We [Pam and Bill] began our tradition journey by choosing a verse that expressed the meaning of our expected baby's name, then inscribing it carefully onto parchment, and framing it to hang outside the baby's room. We wanted our children to know that even before they were born, we prayed God's favor over them. The framed verse served as a daily reminder that God had great plans for them.

In our religious tradition, we have a dedication service and bless our infant at a special church service. Many of our friends have similar traditions of christenings, family baby dedications, and baptisms. Often these traditions are accompanied by family dinners and parties with gifts.

We began another tradition when our children entered preschool or kindergarten. We call it Learner and Leader Day. Each year on that day, we create a fun family activity, then negotiate privileges and responsibilities, and select one leadership trait to focus on the following year for each child. We then choose a verse to pray for that child (which is related to the trait we are focused on), then we give a gift that applauds the unique passion or strength we see God developing in the child's life. In our book *The 10 Best Decisions Every Parent Can Make* (Harvest House, 2006), we explain the details of this event, and have the Learner and Leader chart you can use with your own children. We also select the Learner and Leader gift each year and the gift is best if it is:

- *Practical*, something we might have to buy anyway.
- *Personal*, the child should be able to tell we thought about the gift.
- *Prophetic*, meaning that it speaks the truth about the uniqueness, the *calling*, or the strength we see God building into each child.

(These same components can be integrated if you will be purchasing a gift for your daughter or mentee for her rite of passage.)

When our children enter junior high, we have each of them complete a Relationship Contract (also in *The 10 Best Decisions Every Parent Can Make*) and then we celebrate with that child over dinner. Later, when they are ready to begin to date and drive, we have a special dinner date with the now-young-adult, and we give an ID bracelet and a key chain with the phrase "Until the Day" on one side and 1 Thessalonians 4:3 (NASB) inscribed on the other (this verse reads: "For this is the will of God, your sanctification; that is, that you abstain from sexual immorality"). Our teen's acceptance of the gift is an outward sign of the inward decision he or she has already made to remain chaste until his or her wedding night.

Then, like most families, we have high-school graduation traditions; one of ours includes Mom reading a Bible through, marking it up as a gift. For example, we mark Mom's favorite verses, Dad's favorite verses, verses that have helped us make important decisions, come to salvation, helped us through traumatic times, and so on.

With our sons, either before they leave for college or on their 21st birthday, we have a "Walk into Manhood." For our oldest, we invited his mentors (coaches, favorite teachers, uncles, youth pastor, Student Venture leader, etc.) to the football field (he was a quarterback and going to college on a football scholarship). Each mentor walked the field with our son, explaining what a man is.

Our next son is known for his truck, so a "Drive into Manhood" at a racetrack better fit his personality. The last person to walk (the last man to drive) the final lap was my husband, imparting his final blessing of manhood to our son. Our youngest is aiming at one of the military academies so he is looking forward to a more active tradition, perhaps a "Climb into Manhood" where all the guys will mountain climb and rappel as they share with him.

On our 25th wedding anniversary, Bill and I had a private vow renewal at the chapel on the campus of our alma mater, Biola University. There we read personal vows to one another and Bill pinned our family crest onto our children's jackets. The crest is a symbolic picture of our core family values.

It takes work to create traditions such as the ones you've just read, but it's worth it. To get you started, we'll offer more tips and ideas for family traditions in our next chapter. It was at the wedding of our oldest son that all the traditions (and all the work that went into them) showed the power of their promise. As I watched my husband perform the ceremony where two wide-eyed, excited virgins joined their lives together, a broad smile revealed my grateful heart. All the prayers prayed, all the traditions and gifts given, rolled back through my mind as I heard the words of my new daughter-in-law in her personal wedding vows say to my son, "You are such a man of integrity." As I listened to their vows, and witnessed their "I do's," I thought, *He has become the perfect husband for a daughter of the King of Kings.*

Mentor Moment

I [Pam] asked one of the young women I have mentored for six years to share her story. My relationship with Emily (mentioned earlier in chapter 1) began because of some hurt and pain she needed to deal with from her own family. As mentioned before, her mother, wrapped in her own hurt and pain, was unable to be the helper she needed at that time. (Emily is not her real name.) My role then transitioned from helping to heal her heart to equipping her for her role as a ministry leader. Let's hear from her about the value of a mentor:

I sat across from her at a little café table, sipping my raspberry mocha. I looked into her face, checking her response to each comment I made. Her eyes were attentive, her heart was open; thus began a relationship that forever changed my life. This was the beginning of my discipleship with Pam Farrel. I was a girl from outside her ministry scope, from another town, in desperate need for someone to be Jesus "with skin on" for me. Despite the distance and the reality that I was one more needy person to add to her already full plate, she became that reflection of Jesus I needed.

It wasn't any particular discipleship program, event, or conference that made the difference. It was the way the Lord's love was poured out into my life through Pam. It was her listening ear, genuine concern, sacrificed time and transparency. Pam was one of the first people with whom I had experienced a relationship free from the fear of judgment. I could leave my reservations at the door when I came to meet with her.

Since that first morning we met, Pam has become what I affectionately call my "ministry mom." Through words sprinkled with wisdom and love, she has consistently been available to me through family changes and challenges, ministry hurdles and personal issues. Her husband, Bill, performed our wedding ceremony, and Pam participated too. She has celebrated, supported, and sustained me through the many transitions of my young adult years.

I cannot imagine my life, marriage, or ministry without the precious work the Lord accomplished through Pam. My husband even says that he wouldn't want to see what our marriage would have been like without the healing and growth that God worked through my relationship with her. Needless to say, I am forever grateful to this lovely lady and to our Lord for bending down to meet my heart needs.

Six years forward, my husband and I are in youth and young adult ministry and I find myself surrounded with young women in desperate need for someone to be Jesus "with skin on" for them. I remember that first coffee shop appointment and thank God for the reflection of Jesus that He sent to me.

Look around you. Who has God sent into your life to influence? In truth, in Scripture we are all called to mentor (Titus 2:3–5; 2 Timothy 2:2; Matthew 28:18–20). Are there some future princesses in your world? If not, go find some! Remember, the young women in your world are the future Esthers, Marys, and Miriams who will lead and influence others in powerful ways.

The Power of Our Words

The tongue has the power of life and death. . . .

—Proverbs 18:21

Kind words can be short and easy to speak,

but their echoes are truly endless.

—Mother Teresa

The conversation with the group of young women that day had been one of excitement and laughter as they planned the upcoming special Night of Celebration. Each girl's family would join in a special rite-of-passage ceremony that would culminate with each princess's father reading a personalized blessing over his daughter. However, after the meeting, one princess was not as excited as the rest of the girls, so I [Doreen] initiated a conversation with her.

Darla shrugged her shoulders with frustration as I asked if she would please reconsider asking her father to impart her blessing at the ceremony before she asked her youth pastor. With exasperation she began to blurt out her reasons for not wanting to give her father this privilege: "He spends all his time on that dumb computer! I can tell my parents are not happy. I feel like they might be talking about divorce. I wish he'd spend time with me. I know he used to be a Christian because he used to go to church. I hate being at home. I look for something to do every day just to be away from there."

It was evident that the power of her parents' words—talk of divorce, as well as a lack of loving words—had begun to kill hope in Darla's heart.

My heart grieved for her, knowing also that at just 13 years of age she was already dealing with depression. However, I spoke quickly, reminding her that this might be an opportunity to hear her father publicly say things she never thought he knew or noticed about her. I told her that this would be a day she would remember for the rest of her life and, if possible, it would be best remembered with her father.

Lastly, I asked her if she would allow him this opportunity. She begrudgingly agreed and said she'd let me know of his decision within the next few days. The following day, she called.

"Mrs. Hanna, this is Darla." (Long pause.) "Well, he said yes."

Her tone of voice reflected an irritated disappointment that he had agreed to participate. However, she changed the subject and with excitement told me of the dress a girlfriend was going to let her borrow and how she was looking forward to celebrating with some of her friends.

After we hung up, I called and spoke with Darla's dad, Rick. I explained what he needed to do to prepare to impart her blessing. I sensed sincerity in Rick's voice and felt assured that God was at work.

The night of the ceremony I happened to be standing at the front of the church when Darla and Rick arrived early. As she stepped out of the car, she looked radiant in her beautiful navy blue formal. She ran to find the other girls who were applying their last touches of mascara, lip gloss, or blush. All of them were complimenting and helping each other. In the meantime, Rick had searched and found a parking place, then rushed in asking where he was to sit. I saw that he had a yellow pad of paper in hand. The moment he sat down, it was evident he was still jotting down notes in preparation for Darla's blessing.

The evening moved along smoothly and I soon found myself introducing Darla and Rick. They stepped forward, taking their respective places at the podium. Then Darla folded her arms across her midriff and looked over the heads of the audience. It was so obvious that she was still not happy to be sharing her special moment with her father.

Rick began speaking his blessing with a tone in his voice that reflected tenderness. As Rick's endearing words poured out, Darla's arms soon dropped to her side and she looked directly into her father's eyes. His words were warm,

> *In 15 years, you couldn't*
>
> *find a spare minute to tell*
>
> *me my father's a royal?*
>
> —THE PRINCESS DIARIES

loving, and sincere, bringing life back into Darla's heart. It was evident he truly loved Darla and recognized the importance of this opportunity with his daughter. Darla's eyes filled with tears and a smile brightened her countenance. Rick, with great delight in his eyes, crowned her with her tiara. Then Darla hugged him warmly. You could hear the sniffles of joy in the audience!

As this celebration came to a close and we headed to the reception, I overheard someone affirming Rick, complimenting him for the powerful words he had spoken into Darla's life.

The Fruit Continues

Within a couple of weeks after the celebration, I was more than delighted to see Darla's parents in church together! Several more weeks passed and

I saw Darla's family of five all sitting together on a Sunday morning. I found Darla after church and asked her what had transpired, as I had never seen her dad in church prior to these two occasions.

She excitedly began to share how life had been changing in their home since her celebration. Her dad was no longer spending hours on the computer. She could tell that he and her mother were actually being nicer to each other. And she was thrilled that now her family was going to church together.

I called Darla a year later and asked her to speak at an event to raise money, allowing more girls to experience the joy of being a Modern-Day Princess regardless of their economic background. The evening of the fund-raiser arrived and soon she was sharing about her Night of Celebration. She stated that she had heard things from her dad that she never thought he had even noticed or cared about. With tears of joy she shared of her parents' reconciliation. Home was a place where she used to find any excuse to leave. Within months after the ceremony, she was happy to come home and actually liked staying there—it had become a *place of refuge* (her exact words).

Her excitement shone as she shared that "Dad has taken me out for coffee several times just to talk—it's a miracle. He has even said that he will support me when I go on a mission trip!" she exclaimed.

What a blessing for me to have seen God work so mightily because of a young girl's act of obedience and a father's choice to verbally bless his daughter. Rick's willingness to accept God's call to be the priest of his household and to publicly speak words of blessing upon Darla brought him to a place of reconciliation with Darla, his wife, his two other daughters, and—of greater importance—Jesus Christ.

As we have just seen how the power of Rick's words changed his daughter's heart, remember that the power of your words as a mother, daughter, mentor, father, friend, or whatever your position in life, is influencing the lives of others. And while not every situation will mirror Darla's, we *can* count on God's words to be a "power of life" (Proverbs 18:21); and with our words we will affect the lives of those around us as we speak blessings, not curses, into their lives.

You may be thinking that you've already blown it with your daughter. You've said things you regret. Let me encourage you: Today is a new day. Start fresh and commit to speaking words of truth and blessing into your daughter's life. Your daughter may be hesitant to receive your words at first, but with consistency and perseverance, you can show her that she can trust you to be careful with your words. And by this, you become a model for your daughter to speak righteously to others.

Blesses with Words

It is important to take a few moments to see the history of the power of the spoken word, and how it all got started. Let's go back to the beginning in Genesis 1.

God **said** on the first day, "Let there be light," and there was light (Genesis 1:3). (There it is—the first spoken word!)

God **said** on the third day, "Let the water under the sky be gathered to one place, and let dry ground appear" (Genesis 1:9).

Then on the sixth day God **said**, "Let us make man in our image, in our likeness . . ." (Genesis 1:26).

Take note! The first thing God did with Adam and Eve was to speak a blessing upon them: "God blessed them and said to them, 'Be fruitful and increase in number; fill the earth and subdue it' " (Genesis 1:28).

What an amazing time it must have been for Adam and Eve to enjoy God's presence in the perfect world of the Garden of Eden. They were completely free from fear and they could talk face-to-face with God. Not one bad word was spoken *until* . . .

"Now the serpent was more crafty than any of the wild animals the LORD God had made. He *said* to the woman, 'Did God really say, "You must not eat from any tree in the garden"?' " (Genesis 3:1, emphasis added).

Satan, by his words, twisted God's instructions and created doubt in the mind of Eve. He tempted both Adam and Eve to sin. However, even though they were ushered out of God's perfect environment, God didn't stop communicating with mankind. You might remember a few examples:

- **He spoke** to Noah regarding building the ark in Genesis 6.
- **He spoke** to and through Moses to establish the Ten Commandments in Exodus 20.
- **He spoke** through the prophets of the Old Testament and John the Baptist in the New Testament.
- Most importantly, God sent Jesus to fulfill His Word: "The Word became flesh and made his dwelling among us" (John 1:14).

Throughout Jesus' ministry, words were a powerful part of His effect on the world. Yes, we can quickly recall His amazing miracles and His death and resurrection, but what He said during those times has powerfully influenced the lives of millions of people for more than two thousand years! A few examples of this can be found in the following Bible verses:

- Jesus **said** to His disciples, "Let the little children come to me! Never send them away! For the Kingdom of God belongs to men who have hearts as trusting as these little children's" (Luke 18:16, TLB).
- When He was on the cross He **said**: "Father, forgive them, for they do not know what they are doing" (Luke 23:34).

- Jesus said, "Heaven and earth will pass away, but **my words** will never pass away" (Luke 21:33).
- In His ascension, "While he was **blessing** them, he left them and was taken up into heaven" (Luke 24:51).

I would love to know what words of blessing Jesus spoke over His disciples that day of ascension. Scripture says they returned with great joy to Jerusalem, so I can just imagine what He must have said!

God's written Word reminds us how much God wants to bless us, as well as how we are called to bless others: "Therefore encourage one another and build each other up, just as in fact you are doing" (1 Thessalonians 5:11).

Blessing Prompts Celebration

Webster's Online Thesaurus lists these related terms to "keep" or to "celebrate": honor, praise, BLESS, revere, or consecrate. (Can you believe it? Blessing and celebration are synonymous!)[1] As I [Doreen] was researching the word *celebration* in the Bible, I recognized that all celebration started with and comes from the heart of God. It is evident that our Heavenly Father loves to celebrate and bless His children.

As mentioned earlier, when God created Adam and Eve, He *blessed* them. He celebrated what He had made and wanted many more people to bless, as His blessing was "to be fruitful and multiply." This brings to mind how people experience the joy of newborn babies. We celebrate what has been made in our image, and from that point on, we begin to bless them!

When God brought His people out of Egypt, the first thing He called them to do was to celebrate. And in Exodus 23:14–16, God commanded that His people should keep three celebrations in His honor:

- The first is the Feast of Unleavened Bread—today this is called the Passover. The Passover is still celebrated yearly as a reminder in the Jewish community of their rite of passage. God took them from slavery in Egypt, through the parted waters of the Red Sea, and into the Desert of Shur (freedom).
- The second is the Feast of Harvest, the firstfruits at the beginning of the harvest.
- The third is the Feast of Ingathering, celebrating the bounty gathered at the end of the harvest.

God's heart of celebration is a reminder that we truly must be created in His image, because we, like God, love to party! Isn't it interesting how, between the U.S. government and Hallmark Corporation, they have created many days for us to celebrate?

January:	New Year's Day (It is truly a rite of passage celebrating the step from the old year into the new one.) and Martin Luther King Jr. Day
February:	Presidents Day and Valentine's Day
March:	St. Patrick's Day
April:	Easter (This is another passage—from death to life!)
May:	Mother's Day, Memorial Day, and the National Day of Prayer
June:	Father's Day
July:	Fourth of July (Another passage—from bondage to freedom!)
September:	Labor Day
October:	Halloween (or Harvest Parties) and Boss's Day
November:	Veterans Day and Thanksgiving
December:	Christmas

With a quick search on the Internet, one can find more than three million opportunities to celebrate something. For example, some people celebrate:

- Other people—celebrities like Fred Astaire or Elvis; or they celebrate family heritages, family reunions, volunteers, or heroes.
- Places or events—places like countries, states, or cities; festivals and barbeques; events such as birthdays, weddings, anniversaries, or graduations; personal salvation; and so on.
- Animals or things—animals like frogs, horses, or dogs; the equinox; or new fonts for your computer. There is even a perfume named "Celebrate!"

Some of the "days" people celebrate are hilarious! For example:

- Peculiar People Day (January 10), which is in honor of uniquely different people: unusual, strange, odd, uncommon, intriguing, different, abnormal, or quirky.
- Multiple Personality Day (March 5)—While personality disorders are a serious issue, this holiday has a cute-but-peculiar side. This unique day was brought to our attention by a friend who has overcome this malady, saying, "When you wish someone 'Happy Multiple Personality Day,' you may need to do so multiple times—once for each personality!"
- Wear Something Gaudy Day (October 17) is your chance to really stick out in a crowd. The word "gaudy" refers to something bright, showy, outlandish, or otherwise not in good taste. To have a little fun on this day, people forgo fashion and style, opting for a wild and wacky appearance instead.

Doesn't it seem much more logical to celebrate personal moments in a powerful way that can breathe life into a young person's heart and future? As you grew up, did your cheerleaders in life (family, friends, teachers, and coaches) remember your significant moments with celebration? A new year, a graduation, a birthday, or an anniversary—all such events mark a rite of passage.

Think back in your own life. What word of encouragement or affirmation spoke life and hope into your heart? Was it a comment from your mother? A high-five or "Way to go!" from your dad? A hug and kind whisper from your grandmother or grandfather? Perhaps a teacher or a coach complimented your character or talent? Maybe it was a pastor or youth worker who took the time to give words of encouragement?

Take a moment to jot down 10 nice things that you remember an adult saying to you when you were between the ages of 10 and 21:

1.

2.

3.

4.

5.

6.

7.

8.

9.

10.

If you could list 10, you are fortunate, and you will likely want to repeat the gift of words in the life of a young woman (or women) in your world. If you cannot list 10, you may even more strongly sense the need to be an encouraging adult in the life of a young woman. You can offer words of affirmation and set up opportunities for others to give her powerful, life-giving words of encouragement, too.

In addition, for many young women, the first prom serves as a pseudo–rite of passage, and we relegate this vital duty to a 14- to 18-year-old boy who may or may not have the best interest of the "princess" in mind. How much more valuable it is to celebrate a young woman's life through a rite-of-passage experience and celebration ceremony in the company of adults, leaders, and friends speaking truth and encouragement to her.

> *A word fitly spoken and in due season is like apples of gold in settings of silver.*
>
> —Proverbs 25:11, AMP

We believe it is in the nature of every culture to celebrate significant moments in life. A ceremony defines a moment and helps a young woman embrace her family, church, and friends who will come alongside her as she ventures into her future. A ceremony also solidifies her decisions and requires accountability—both are key in holding her to her commitment to live as a daughter of the King. We'll talk a little more in-depth about the rite-of-passage ceremony in chapter 7.

Traditions of Affirmation

A teenage girl will see a rite-of-passage celebration and a blessing as a natural and normal activity if you can weave encouragement into her life on a regular basis. Look for times, places, and opportunities to share encouraging, affirming, and inspiring words with your daughter. Following are a few ideas real moms and dads have created to set an atmosphere where words of affirmation and moments of celebration can be shared. See which of these traditions might work for your family!

On a Nightly Basis: Our [the Farrel] family prays at every meal, and every night before bed we pray with each child and bless and affirm his character and choices. Then each child prays to thank God for the day. Lane Jordan, author of *12 Steps to Becoming a More Organized Mom,* added her twist to this ritual and writes:

> The one thing I did that created a tradition was to carve out time each evening and read to my daughters. With the age difference of the girls, I had to do this reading two times. So I remember having to make a crucial decision between that and television. I am so thankful God gave me the desire to do the reading! The result of this special time together gave us the time to talk, to bond, and to give them the head knowledge and heart longing for God's Word as well as for great literature.
>
> The girls "let" me read to them until they were 15 years old! With their heads on my shoulder or in my lap, I was able to have the physical contact that I believe so many mothers yearn for from their children. I also believe that this time helped them to stay on the right path from so many of the destructive choices that are in our world today.[2]

[Note from authors: This kind of tradition sets up a daily time of natural, open sharing and affirmation between a parent and teen daughter—even after the "reading" time might come to an end.]

On the First Date: Ron and Gina work with youth through Teen Impact ministry. (Ron mentored two of the Farrel boys in high school.) Gina shares this idea: "When Petra and Paige (our daughters) went on their first dates, Ron gave them each a 'Celebration' present. He gave them each a cross necklace and told them how much he respected them for honoring their contracts and going on their first dates with growing Christian men."

On a Pivotal Birthday: Television personality Christie Rayburn, co-host of *Marriage Uncensored with Dave and Christie,* created a rite of passage of the "feminine kind" for her daughter Taylor on the day she turned 13. The centerpiece of the table at that celebration was 12 white candles and one pink one.

Colossians 3 was selected as Taylor's life Scripture passage, and that set of verses was framed and was part of the centerpiece. Christie had invited key women in Taylor's life to the celebration, and beforehand, she had given each woman a character trait to focus on. That trait was to be the focus of some words of wisdom prepared to share with Taylor.

At the celebration birthday party, first, Christie shared the privilege of being Taylor's mom, and all the roles she had played in Taylor's life (teacher, disciplinarian, spiritual advisor, etc.). Christie then invited each woman to share the trait and any words of wisdom she had for Taylor. Each woman spoke truth into Taylor's life and committed to continue to be a positive influence, mentor, and role model for Taylor.

The celebration continued as Christie would introduce the next trait of a godly woman, and one by one, the invited guests were encouraged to speak into Taylor's life. Christie then explained to Taylor that as she transitioned into her 13th year, she would be taking on the responsibility for growing and developing her own life, and that Christie's role was now shifting.

Christie concluded the ceremony as she blew out the 12 white candles and Taylor was asked to light the one pink candle, signifying she accepted the responsibility of womanhood. Then this gathering of women prayed and enjoyed each other's company and desserts together. Christie plans to invite these same women back to celebrate Taylor as she crosses into adulthood at 18 as well.[3]

Annetta E. Dellinger, an author known as a "Joyologist," creates memories for her family with a dash of laughter and a splash of encouragement. "On our daughter's 13th birthday, she got 13 of her favorite foods to eat. She received a box with 13 little gifts (lotions, brushes, candy, etc., and one special item she requested) to open one each day for 13 days."

[Authors' note: You can add 13 cards of encouragement, 13 words that describe her, or other affirmations to bless your daughter.]

Pre-Graduation: Annetta describes what became a new family tradition: "On the Christmas before spring graduation, I went back through all her school pictures and made photocopies of different ones, which were then used as name tags on everyone's gifts. Each person passed their gift around before opening and made silly and serious comments about their memories of the picture. What a fun night of memories! I also secretly learned her favorite foods and served them for our family Christmas dinner. From that date on the rest of the kids wanted the same treatment!"[4]

> *Words of affirmation are what create the most memorable celebrations in the heart of the recipient.*
>
> —Doreen Hanna

Annetta knows the secret of opening a heart—joy. A little laughter can set a loving atmosphere that prepares a heart to receive the more serious words when given. Laughter, because it releases endorphins, helps energize and embed a shared moment into the memory.

On Her Spiritual Birthday: Pastor's wife Cindy McMenamin shares a tradition her family did for her daughter, Dana, on the yearly anniversary of when she began a relationship with Christ. Cindy explains:

Early on in Dana's younger years we established a tradition of recognizing her 're-birthday'—the anniversary of the day she first gave her life to Christ. So on her first re-birthday at age eight, I gave her a "blessing" bracelet (what most people call a charm bracelet) and each year would add another "charm" to represent a blessing that she has in Christ.

Eventually, she got the charms at certain occasions that I wanted her to remember, with a heart of gratitude to God for making that occasion possible. For instance, at her first piano recital, she got a little silver piano charm to place on her blessing bracelet, to remind her of the musical ability God blessed her with.

After spending a weekend with her in Palm Springs, she got a little palm tree charm for the bracelet, as a reminder to thank God that we were able to have that weekend. When she turned 12, the "blessing" on her bracelet was a little cheetah purse that symbolized the "riches" she has in Christ. The bracelet, now full of blessings, is a keepsake that she often shows others as she recounts what God has blessed her with.[5]

To Share a Vision of Purity: Gina Rackley's girls received purity rings on their 13th birthdays after completing the Relationship Contract created by Pam and Bill Farrel. Gina shares, "Petra lost her ring during her junior year in high school at a track meet. She had put it into her pocket right before her hurdle race and when she took her sweats off, she lost it. She was devastated and crying because she knew that we would never find that little ring in that huge football field. So, we stopped and prayed and trusted that it would show up. We walked up and down the field with her friends looking but found nothing.

"At the very end of the meet, a mom from the other team came up to Ron (who was coaching at the time), not knowing that Ron was Petra's dad or that she had lost her ring, and told him that she had found this ring. Petra saw the faithfulness of the Lord and how He answers prayer."

Beginning the summer when a daughter is 13, each Rackley daughter also reads *Preparing for Adolescence* by Dr. James Dobson, with her parents; then each summer after, the daughter is assigned an additional relationship or character-building book.

Dana's parents gave her a purity ring at age 16 with a little more panache. Since Dana is active in music and dance, her Sweet 16 was a "Hollywood" night complete with a "movie" (PowerPoint of still pictures and video) of Dana's life set to a favorite Christian song and a live band from her Christian school that played favorite tunes. Dana was released to date by her dad after receiving her purity ring.

To Give Back: Author Nancy Sebastian Meyer writes, "For our daughter's high school graduation party, we are in the midst of planning a special dinner to honor the people who have been instrumental in teaching and mentoring Becky throughout her life. In this way, she is celebrating *their* accomplishments and thanking them for the gifts they have already given her by giving them appreciation. This, we feel, is a good way to transition her from being in the spotlight to giving back to those who built into her life."[6]

On a Tough Day: Nancy also knew the beginning of menses is a hard day for most girls so she planned to do something special with her daughter whenever that day appeared: "I wanted to make it a positive celebration rather than allow it to be something to fear getting—or not getting—as soon as all the other girls. So I promised Becky that regardless of the day, when her period came we would take off and share a 'girl's day out' complete with ear piercing (for which she had begged a long time).

"On the special day, we skipped school to celebrate with the earrings, a makeover at the mall, lunch at a fun restaurant, and a game of miniature golf—all to make her feel really good about being a woman with additional responsibilities."[7]

With Dad: Rich Meyer (Nancy Sebastian Meyer's husband) has a tradition of taking his daughter out for breakfast on the first day of school, then giving her a new charm for her charm bracelet, along with some words of encouragement to launch her year.

To Remember: When my sons and nieces and nephews were small, we [the Farrel family] had more than one Christmas when money was tight. One year I felt God tell me, "Then write them a story." So I created a children's story where the punch line at the end was "and the angel is YOU!" Then each child was given an angel-shaped ornament (made of paper!) and the child was placed in the center of the extended family circle where everyone would say something nice about that child, and it was recorded on the ornament.

When the boys were all teens, we took one Christmas to reread what people said about them to remind them of all the good others saw in them. When fiancées and wives began to enter our family, we again pulled out the ornaments to read and rejoice to see how many words of blessing had actually come true through the Lord's power in each of their lives.

If your own daughter is still very young, you might consider tweaking this Christmas tradition and each Christmas give her a "crown" or princess ornament (or any ornament that would hold special meaning for your daughter) and tie to it a new positive trait or area of growth you have seen in her life. By the year of her rite of passage, many tiaras will be sprinkled through your Christmas tree, and perhaps these can be wrapped and given to her the night of her rite-of-passage celebration, as she graduates high school, at her wedding shower, or as a gift for her to begin her own tree and her own affirming celebrations as she forms a new family.

Creating Ways to Mark the Important Days

Dr. Catherine Hart Weber comes from a rich heritage. Her father is Dr. Archibald Hart, a best-selling author and frequent guest on Focus on the Family radio. Her mother, Kathleen Hart, is a professor and leader among clergy wives. Catherine is a woman with a priority and conviction of celebrating life's meaningful moments. She shares here some of the traditions she and her daughters have created. As you scroll through these ideas, ask yourself, *What is the next teachable moment or transition in my daughter's life, and how can I add affirmation and encouragement to that moment?* Let's hear from Dr. Weber how and why celebrating is a good idea:

> There were several moments worth marking in my girls' lives as they developed. Some were thoughtfully planned out, and others were more spontaneous, as they happened.
>
> Celebrating firsts and intentionally marking transitions are important landmarks in a girl's development. They are like building altars of remembrance to reflect back on. Celebrating with rituals and traditions has significant impact on each stage of a girl's development, especially when her mother and father and other close family and friends are positively involved. (Gathering family and friends at significant moments affirms the positive events and phases of a girl's development, launching her into the next stage.)
>
> Some of the more significant birthdays were 10, 13, 16, 18, and 21:

- 10 because you are now double digits.
- 13 because you are now a teenager.
- 16 because you can legally drive.
- 18 because you are now able to vote and have some adult privileges.
- 21 because you are usually considered an adult.

Besides birthdays, it is important to celebrate all firsts and special occasions in a girl's life, such as going off to school, getting your period (becoming a woman), going to your first dance, the prom, graduations, and any other accomplishment or special occasion in their eyes.

You only pass by once, and these are landmarks of memories and opportunities to impact positively as each experience passes by. Stop and notice. Savor the moments. Celebrate with her. Bake a cake. Gather family and friends for a party. Give a card. Write a special note. Give a meaningful gift. Take her out for a special occasion. Take photos and videos. Make photo albums. Let her get dressed up—and get nails, hair, and makeup done. Talk with her about each landmark. Listen to how it made her feel and what it means to her.

I [Dr. Weber] have realized over the years just how important it is that we listen to the hearts of our daughters, and get our clues from them, to set the pace and find what is most meaningful for celebrating rituals and marking moments—at the time. Imposing our expectations or ideals on marking the moments for our daughters is not the most loving response.

Be sensitive to your daughter's personality, her heart, and what would be most meaningful to her. It doesn't matter what would be 'ideal,' what others have done, what your other daughters have done, what you did, or what has been done for generations. Marking the moment meaningfully will only be a true celebration to be remembered if it is meaningful to your daughter. As moms, we need to remember: It's not about us. It's about her. It's about marking the moments and milestones in her life journey. Let's take a closer look at some of those milestones.

Birthdays. On my eldest daughter's 10th birthday, we rented the roller-skating rink, and invited all the friends and family we could think of.

For our daughters' 16th, they each got to choose something significant as their way to celebrate. Their father gave them both a piece of Tiffany jewelry. One chose a promise ring and the other chose a promise bracelet instead. He had a special date with them, and marked the significant time in their life. We also made a big deal when they could drive on their own.

For the 18th, it's off to the spa. That is when you can legally have a massage (in the state we live in), so it's a chance to do something new. Their dad gave them another significant piece of jewelry from Tiffany's.

Becoming a woman. The 'becoming a woman' transition usually comes as a surprise. Often neither mother nor daughter is prepared. For both my daughters, their official 'womanhood' came unannounced. When one of my daughters was in fifth grade, I got a frantic call from the school. During the day, she was bothered by stomach pains, and then had to excuse herself during class to go to the bathroom. When she returned, there was some whispering and tones of 'drama' with her friends.

When I arrived at the school, I got wind of the rumors that

were spreading among the boys. One announced that she had started her 'masturcation' which was refuted by another more knowledgeable boy who stated she had started her 'womanly thing' which was 'white stuff' coming out of her. Needless to say, there were some confused little fifth graders, not at all prepared for this rite of passage. It is coming sooner for young girls these days, often before they even want to know about all these details.

The onset was a shock and somewhat traumatic for my daughter and me. This made it even more important to mark the transition. At first she was resistant to making a big deal about it. She felt shamed and needed time to process the jolt and all the implications. After a few days, it slowly settled in, and we talked more about it, and then began to celebrate the wonder of the beginning of 'womanhood'—ever so gently and appropriately for yet still a 'child.'

There is no one right way to celebrate becoming a woman, especially when you are just a child. It is different for each girl. As a mom, I learned with my first daughter that you need to be sensitive to what is meaningful to the child, depending on her age and the circumstances. Let her set the pace and give the clues for what will best mark the moment.

I had thought about how I would mark 'the moment,' and had a pre-conceived plan in place. However, the sudden onset and the somewhat stressful circumstances threw my whole fantasy off. I had planned to go to tea with some family and friends. To share the moment and do something 'ladies' would do. Instead, I had to be sensitive to process my daughter's unexpected embarrassment and the repercussions of the social and personal adjustment for her.

It's common that young girls don't want to talk about it or make a big deal about it. They need time to process the changes in their body; so, responding to what she seemed to need, I gave her some space and went slowly, starting with logistics. "Would you like to go to the drugstore and pick out some pads that you would like? Would you like to put together a special bag for your personal items that you can keep in your backpack?"

I only talked about what she was comfortable with and was sensitive to go at her pace. Over a few weeks and the next time round, she was a little more comfortable talking about it. I took my cues from her.

Graduations. For my eldest daughter's eighth-grade graduation, we hosted a party for the entire class. We opened up our home, and cleared out the living room and converted it into a karaoke party room. We rented a deejay with disco lights and had lots of food. The kids broke off into small groups and worked up routines together to the karaoke songs. They had so much fun, and so did the adult chaperones.

For high-school graduation, we had a family party with cards and presents and gave the gift-of-a-lifetime gym membership and another piece of Tiffany jewelry.

Turning 21. This marks the close of the last stage of development and rite of passage for a 'child,' a more significant launching, dividing the line between teen and adult. This ritual is for the parents as much as for the child. Your baby is now officially an adult—whatever that entails.

I remember when I turned 21. My dad and I went out to lunch, and I asked if I could call him Arch—seeing as we were both now adults. Well, that lasted about as long as the lunch did. But it was a ritual that seemed to capture many elements of the rite of passage.

A tradition from generations in South Africa, where I grew up, is to give a '21 key' signifying you now hold the 'key' to the rest of your adult life. It is also the time to begin a 'hope chest,' giving gifts that would contribute to establishing your own home and adult life.[8]

In my [Pam's] book *Got Teens?*, written with Hearts at Home founder Jill Savage, we share a few more ideas for family traditions:

Terrific 12. You might be able to beat your daughter to the starting line of womanhood by making her 12th birthday packed with firsts. (For some early bloomers, you might need to move this up a year and do a "Double Digits" party at 11.) Buy her first razor to shave her legs, her first set of high heels, or her first makeup set; take her to have her ears pierced or whatever next step you feel is age appropriate for your family.

Sweet 16. Try one of these ideas to mark this big moment (or adapt it to whenever you feel she is ready to date):

- On the Town: Host a formal dinner party where her closest friends (guys and gals) dress to the nines and eat the fanciest gourmet food you can afford. Play classical music, or hire a harpist or a string quartet.
- Dance the Night Away: Host a dance, one where couples learn some classics, like the waltz, swing, tango, and two-step. You will have to spring for a band, dance instructor, and food, but it will definitely be a memory.

- High Tea: Take her and a few of her closest friends (and maybe their moms or all the female relatives) to high tea. Bring along photos of her growing up years—and yours. Hand down a piece of jewelry that has been in the family for a couple of generations.
- Passport 2 Purity: As she enters her teen years, take her away for a special weekend with Mom. Using FamilyLife's "Passport 2 Purity" resource, discuss her changing body and the new season of life she is entering. Take some time to go shopping and have some special girl time to mark this transition in her life. (Passport 2 Purity can also be used with your teen son.)[9]

If we give the gift of words wrapped in creative tradition, one day those words will boomerang back to bless us, as author Linda Newton discovered:

I have two beautiful daughters. They arrived bringing flights of fancy with fairy princesses, dollhouses, and our personal favorite—tea parties. I bought my oldest daughter, Sarah, her first tea set on her third birthday. That same day we filled the tiny plastic teapot with sweet tea, made bologna sandwiches with the crust cut off, and served banana chips with a dollop of peanut butter—Sarah's favorite. Then we sipped tea and chatted about the clouds, the flower garden, and our new puppy. Life couldn't get any better.

When Sarah was five, she was joined by a baby sister. Ashley was barely old enough to hold a teacup when she was invited to join us. And the three of us drank our tea with delight even though Ashley's table manners at the time left much to be desired.

As the years progressed so did the tea parties. Bologna sandwiches gave way to cream cheese and cucumber. Sweet tea was replaced by loose-leaf tea we found at various specialty shops. The conversations evolved as well. We now discussed hairstyles and friendships—important things in the life of teenagers.

The girls grew and Sarah married and moved out. About that time a teahouse opened in our little town. No more plastic dishes or paper plates for us; we had the real deal. At least once a month I'd pick Ashley up after high school and we'd head over for tea and scones in the early afternoon. Many times we were the only ones in the place.

Time stood still as Ashley and I talked about her future plans, kids in her class making heart-breaking choices, or whether Sarah's husband was going to be okay while he was stationed in Iraq. Those were deep and precious moments to be treasured.

Ashley, too, grew up and headed off to college. One year during spring break, I was blessed to have both girls home at the same time, Sarah from graduate school and Ashley from her second year at the university. This was a rare moment for us so I headed off to the grocery store to purchase our Easter feast.

When I returned the girls motioned for me to follow them out to the deck. There was the patio table set with my fine china, complete with linen tablecloth and napkins. The table was laden with cucumber and cream cheese sandwiches and completed with banana chips frosted with peanut butter. The girls poured our Blue Lady tea and we laughed and talked until the sun set. I felt so honored that of all the places my beautiful girls could be on that spring break, they chose to be with me. Apparently I wasn't the only one who valued those treasured moments over tea.[10]

It will take a little effort, a little time, a little energy, but you can create unique and personalized moments where the gift of words can be given that will breathe life, hope, healing, and love into your daughter's future. Words are the gift every person can afford to give—and the gift a young woman most needs to receive.

Mentoring Moment

I [Pam] could hardly wait for seventh period! It was the last hour of the day in my junior-high schedule. Mrs. Clough was my favorite teacher. She would read from a novel for 15 minutes in each class, and those minutes seemed magical as they transported me to faraway countries, and lives that seemed far more exciting than the simple life of an Idaho farm girl.

But it was the classwork we did, diagramming sentences, that I looked forward to most. The majority of the class would groan as Mrs. Clough would instruct us to take out our grammar books, but I loved this moment. Mrs. Clough would ask for volunteers to come to the chalkboard and diagram a sentence, artfully drawing out the subject, verb, noun, prepositional phrases, and so on. I loved the work, but what I loved more were Mrs. Clough's words of encouragement, "Pam, you can do these so quickly. You really have a knack for this! I wonder if there is a writer in you."

The days I loved most were the days when some students wanted to hide in the bathroom or fake a stomachache to get a pass to the nurse's office. Those were the afternoons we'd write in class, and then stand in front of the class and

read our work aloud. As other classmates ducked for cover,
praying Mrs. Clough wouldn't call on them, my hand would fly up
to volunteer. Mrs. Clough could be counted on to give the words
I longed to hear, "Pam, I believe there is a book or two in that
heart of yours. Wouldn't surprise me if I one day will check out
a book that you have written from our very own library!"

They were simple words. I am sure she must have said similar things to hundreds of students over her lifetime of teaching at that same junior-high school, but those words spoke life
into my heart. I always loved to read, but after Mrs. Clough
got a hold on my heart, I read voraciously, checking out several
books—more than 300 or 400 pages long—at a time. I had to
convince the librarian I could indeed read that many books in a
two-week period.

I look back and I wonder what my life would be like today if
I had not had the blessing and God-ordained privilege of having
Mrs. Clough as my first writing mentor. She didn't spend hours
and hours of extra time with me—though she'd read anything
I wrote and brought to her. She didn't fawn over my talent
and press me into summer college classes or encourage my
parents to send me to a writing camp. No, her influence was
simple. She gave a sentence or two of truthful encouragement
every day for nine months, and within that year, a writer was
born.

So often, as adults, we feel we don't have enough time
or training to be a mentor. We might feel our words lack
eloquence—but that is the wonder of mentoring. Simple
phrases of truth, aptly spoken, are like the two fish and those

few loaves that the disciples gathered from a little boy's lunch that fed the five thousand. When we give our small, simple part, God adds Himself and a miracle happens, and people are fed. When you give whatever time you have available, and speak whatever words God brings to your mind, young women's lives will be changed for eternity.

In that little library, in that rural community, there are books with that young woman's name on the spine. To date, I have written 30 titles, but it all began with a little seed of kindness that was planted by Mrs. Clough.

The Journey to Her Celebration

Cultivate inner beauty, the gentle,
gracious kind that God delights in.

—1 PETER 3:4 (MSG)

The road to love may be barred by still many more dangers,
which you alone will have to face. So arm yourself with this
enchanted Shield of Virtue, and this mighty Sword of Truth,
for these weapons of righteousness will triumph over evil.

—SLEEPING BEAUTY (1959)

*E*very teenage girl seeks to understand how she can become a success-ful woman, a woman of influence and wisdom. As a mother or mentor, it will be your joy and honor to provide opportunities for her to discover many things that will enable her to see herself spiritually as a daughter of the King.

We've already recognized that there seems to be a process that is important in the maturing of every teen girl, regardless of her cultural upbringing. I [Doreen] believe this has come from the wisdom of generations, recognizing that times change but human nature does not. As the founder of Treasured Celebrations and the creator of the DOK and MDP programs, I have garnered the core information needed in preparing a teenage girl for the special moment that acknowledges her step from adolescence into womanhood.

I believe the steps in this chapter are necessary to help her become a well-rounded young lady. You can tailor the topics to fit your family schedule and weave them into already-established mother/daughter moments, or you can use the *Becoming a Modern-Day Princess Journal* and gather a few of your daughter's friends, or you can launch a small group using this material in your church or civic group. The format and pace might vary, depending on how much time you have available or how in-depth you choose to cover the material; however, eight topics of value are mentioned here in this chapter. (The *Becoming a Modern-Day Princess Journal* covers the following topics as well.)

For some moms, it might be easier for the material to be spread over several months with once-a-month mom/daughter dates, or used on a weekend away with your princess. It is highly flexible material so use it as you see best to fit your family schedule, goals, and lifestyle.

From my [Pam's] lifetime of mentoring young women and in leadership in women's ministry, I concur that there is a series of steps, a ladder of input if you will, that transitions a teen girl into a young woman of influence. As you take your daughter through this journey, you will witness firsthand the profound positive effect on her life, or if you are a mentor, you will see it in the lives of your girls as they traverse this vital material.

Personality and Affirmation

One of the key components in beginning this journey is to enable your daughter (or the teen girls you hope to influence) to discover and understand her God-given personality traits and character qualities. I [Doreen] believe that a personality profile is very beneficial for accomplishing the first half of this. Girls giggle with delight as they dive into the treasure chest full of traits and qualities that make them uniquely who they are.

The young woman discovers her strengths, finds out if she is more people-oriented or task-oriented, more introverted or extroverted, and learns how to maximize her strengths and minimize her weaknesses. (See the Recommended Resources pages for tools to help with this exercise.)

Complementing the self-discovery profile is an exercise that personally affirms her character and value. When I take a young woman through her preparation process, I use three cards that are given to three trusted adults who are willing to write a note of affirmation to her. As a mother or a mentor, present those three cards, along with a note of instruction, to the individuals who have agreed to write words of affirmation. The note of instruction will request that each of these willing adults write about one personality or character trait that they love about this young lady and then return the card to her sealed in the envelope that has also been provided.

The anticipation of opening and reading aloud these affirmation notes is one of the most powerful parts of her journey. The personal notes from respected adults quickly demonstrate that others do love certain things about her, often bringing many joyful tears from this simple but compelling exercise. Hearing words of affirmation can make all the difference to a young woman who may be dealing with feelings of insecurity or a lack of self-esteem during this in-between stage.

Another key aspect of self-discovery involves broadening her view of her family. This program provides an opportunity for a girl to define her ethnic background and find out about her family heritage by hearing family stories that have been passed down. In the Appendix you'll find a "Family Legacy Worksheet" to give your daughter. As your daughter fills out the worksheet, consider pulling out family albums or scanning through family photos, taking the time to talk about each family member and share how each person has influenced your family—positively or negatively. Talking openly about family history helps a young woman access the positive and negative aspects of the legacy that has been handed to her, so she can decide which to repeat and which to replace. This also helps her begin the adult task of asking, "How can I build on what has been given to me?"

This is also a time to discover the meaning of her first name and possibly investigating its spiritual meaning. A quick Internet search will give you a list of places to discover the meanings of different names.

> *But I think she might*
>
> *be a real princess!*
>
> —ENCHANTED

This is an exciting discovery because the girl will often see how perfectly her name aligns with her personality or character traits. Other times she may see that her name is something she will grow to become. Doreen is a version of Dorothea, which means "gift of God." It has created a pretty lofty goal for me to strive for! Pamela means "sweeter than honey" and when I [Pam] learned that, I wanted to become a person who was other-centered.

Seeing a rich family heritage accompanied with uncovering the meaning of her name adds another layer of confidence to the developing young woman.

Character Development

Building character during this journey is very important. As teenage girls, one of their greatest challenges is choosing obedience in their spiritual walk with God. Therefore, it is necessary to spend time talking about the rewards of obedience at this juncture of their lives. Leading a young woman to discover her inner heart for God is the key that will open up her future and place her under God's umbrella of favor. Everyone wants to have a blessed life. A young woman of integrity understands that blessing comes when one is obedient to her Heavenly Father.

Discussions about character should touch on the importance of honesty (being truthful in word and deed); discernment (exercising good judgment); faithfulness (keeping your promises and commitments to others); trust (using discretion when someone shares private thoughts or information with you); and righteousness (living a life that is exemplary and above reproach). A great resource to foster this discussion is the book of Ruth. Have your daughter count the many times Ruth chose to be obedient, and ask her to recount the historical rewards Ruth received from her actions.

Also have her look at the tough decisions Ruth had to make in each chapter and talk about how a young woman can learn to make wise choices. A mature young woman has learned the balance of respecting legitimate authority and learning to take responsibility over her own choices and decisions. In my [Pam's] Bible, in the margins of the book of Ruth I've written:

- Chapter 1: Ruth made a great decision. What was it?
- Chapter 2: Ruth is known as a great woman. Why? What traits does she have that make her a great person?
- Chapter 3: Boaz is a great man. What does he do to show he is a great person? What are his choices?
- Chapter 4: There is a great reward. How did God honor these people for making such wise decisions?

Feel free to share these questions with your daughter as you delve into the book of Ruth. The decision to follow God wholeheartedly can completely transform the future of a teen girl. I [Doreen] and other Modern-Day Princess small-group leaders have witnessed some dramatic transformations, such as the one below:

"By the grace of God I am what I am," (1 Corinthians 15:10). I love that verse because I know if it wasn't for God's grace, I would not be who I am today. I fear where I would be today without the amazing transformation that happened in my life through my rite of passage.

Up until last year I thought I was content and happy. I was having "fun" even if I felt miserable days afterwards. I was a "church-going Christian" who only lived for myself. Often, I would leave church to get high. I loved the feeling of that high and I would do anything I had to get it. There were times when I woke up not knowing what had happened the night before, having had sex with different guys. That got me into a lot of sticky situations, as you can probably imagine.

I was on probation all of my 15th year of life and last summer I went to my last party and did my last round of drugs. I was celebrating getting off of probation and being able to break the law again. That was my last and worst high. I don't know what happened. I just remember that I felt miserable, my emotions were going crazy. I think that's when I felt I couldn't hide the pain anymore of what was really going on in my soul, and I saw how ugly my life was without Jesus.

I felt all of the pain that I had brought on myself. That's when I knew something had to happen in my life.

I didn't know it was going to be through my rite of passage.
I wasn't going to do it. There was a battle going on in my head
just for me to sign this little piece of paper, which really was me
saying "I want change." If you had asked me a year ago who I was
I would have just said, "I am trying to find myself."

Today I'll tell you that I'm a daughter of the King. I know
I matter in heaven and that God has given me purpose in this
world. Even if it's just to give someone a hug or an encouraging
word. Whatever it might be, I know God can use me, and that
who I was doesn't define who I am today. I know that my past is
over and my future is secure. I know that God is always there and
that He never leaves my side.

Even in hard times, I still know "God is who He is no matter
where I am." I still stumble sometimes but I don't sit and wallow
in my mistakes. I get up, I repent, and I keep moving forward. I
have wasted enough time. I made a pact to live for God and not
turn back, and I'm sticking to it.

Oh, one last thing, I used to be a cutter. When I was still "out
there," I had written the word "whore" on my leg with a knife
and you could still sort of see the word even though I had written
it over a year ago. However, recently I was looking for the scars
and they weren't there anymore. I felt like God said to me, "That's
because I've healed you."

—Valerie

[Note from Doreen: This young lady has truly become a young woman
of integrity. Today, she leads an alumnae group that assists the facilitator
with each upcoming group of future Modern-Day Princesses.]

Learning the Value of True Friends

At this point in the lives of teen girls, friendship is usually paramount, or moving in that direction. Oftentimes teen girls listen more to their friends' opinions than their parents. Peer pressure becomes more and more of a factor in a young woman's life. For these reasons, it's crucial to emphasize to her the importance of her choice of friends and the power of influence. The Bible challenges all of us to make a clear-cut decision:

> Do not be misled: "Bad company corrupts good character."
>   (1 Corinthians 15:33)

> Blessed is the man [young woman]
>   who does not walk in the counsel of the wicked
>   or stand in the way of sinners
>   or sit in the seat of mockers.
> But [her] delight is in the law of the LORD,
>   and on his law [she] meditates day and night.
> [She] is like a tree planted by streams of water,
>   which yields its fruit in season
>   and whose leaf does not wither.
> Whatever [she] does prospers. (Psalm 1:1–3)

Surrounding herself with quality friends will help your daughter make wiser choices. Spend some time with her discussing the qualities she believes are important in a true friend. Then ask her if she is living out the kind of character qualities that she is looking for in others. Provide examples, good and bad, of how different friends have affected your life and have her share the same.

One of the strongest reasons to implement a rite of passage with a small group of girls is to provide the time and opportunity for them to meet one another and create quality friendships with girls who will help and encourage them to make wise choices. And for those moms planning a family-sponsored rite-of-passage journey, in the Appendix is a "Friendship Evaluation Worksheet," which is a resource that can be a great addition to your conversation about friends. It can also be adapted for use as a discussion starter in a Becoming a Modern-Day Princess small group.

Let's hear an example of how having positive friendships can influence a young woman:

In the "Value of True Friends" class we were given the assignment to watch our friends and find out who is a true friend. For the next couple weeks I just watched and listened. My senior prom was coming up very soon and we all had plans to go together as a big group. As I listened, I realized that my friends and I did not have the same plan for prom night.

They were making it their mission to get me "messed up." My best friend said nothing in my defense but instead laughed with them. How could I call these people my friends? I could not stay friends with those people anymore.

The next week our assignment for the week was to journal our feelings in the morning and again in the evening, seeing if we had acted on our feelings or gave our day to God. Journaling my feelings really helped me see that I put too much into my bad friends instead of trusting God to guide me. The closer I got with God, the farther away I felt from my best friend, it hurt so much.

I thought I could fix my friends and their problems. I

thought I could do everything! That was the biggest lie I told myself, and this class made me realize that it's God's job to be God, not mine. I can put my trust in Him and all His promises because He's never let me down.

—Carina

Pursuing Knowledge

Teenage girls are like sponges and they pursue knowledge by nature. They always seem ready to learn new things. Today's technology provides them with everything they would ever want to know—both good and bad—so they need to build an internal filter to help them build discernment in their trek for wisdom and knowledge.

Spend time discussing what they already know and who helped them learn it. Ask them if the source was reliable. Affirm the value of others God has brought into their lives to help them acquire the information, knowledge, and wisdom they have accumulated thus far. Follow that discussion by addressing where and whom they are going to seek for answers about their future pursuits and decisions.

> *Knowledge is love and light and vision.*
>
> —Helen Keller

During this part of the journey, provide your daughter (or mentees) the opportunity to affirm others. Have her write a love note to her mother (or a woman she respects), her father (or the man who will affirm her), and also to her friends, stating in each note a character quality she appreciates in the person she is writing to.

Some mothers or mentors have also arranged community projects during this time to help the girls see the rewards of giving time, talents, or even treasure (monetary donations). Serving others is a terrific way to show young women that in giving they receive. She might receive new mentors, new opportunities, new skills, new knowledge—all from giving a little of herself away.

A few practical ideas for service opportunities include:

- Serving meals at a soup kitchen
- Organizing a food drive through your church or community
- Getting a group of friends together to host a free car-wash for the community
- Cleaning out closets and taking any clothes, coats, or shoes that aren't being used to a shelter or thrift shop
- Spending an afternoon visiting residents at a nursing home
- Cooking a meal for a family going through a difficult time
- Babysitting (at no charge) for a couple who could use a night out

Etiquette and Makeup

Another aspect of affirming a girl's womanhood is training her in appropriate table etiquette and incorporating natural beauty tips. This, of course, is always a highlight of the journey. This can be a fun mom/daughter date, something a group of friends and their moms do together, or a Becoming a Modern-Day Princess group event. There are many resources on the Internet or at the library that provide an education in both of these arenas. You'll also find some resource recommendations in the back of the book.

There may also be a refined woman, or older college woman, who is talented in this area who would be willing to give input and help. Enhancing their outward beauty is very important to teenage girls at this season of their lives. A mother, mentor, or leader can use the platform of developing a princess's outer beauty as a segue to a discussion on the importance of inner beauty. Each princess can then grasp the opportunity to make choices to develop her inner beauty. Etiquette training enables a teen girl to act like a princess; makeup enables her to look and feel like one!

Here is a reflection by one leader who participated in this part of the program:

> I have had the privilege of being part of two rites of passage in the last two years as an assistant facilitator. I have served during the makeup and manners night four separate times. Being a part of the makeup and manners night was right up my alley.
>
> I have had my hands in makeup since I was three years old, and my hands, I guess, just never came out. The manners part would later follow when I started auditioning for pageants, interviewing for jobs, and meeting influential people. So needless to say, this night was one of my favorites and I loved teaching the girls how to apply makeup and behave like a lady. Although I realized the importance of this night, my eyes were opened the night of the crowning ceremony.
>
> I saw that all the weeks preparing for this night were like the night Esther prepared to stand before the king. The doors opened, and the princesses walked down the aisle. The time came at the end of the blessing when the fathers placed their crowns on their daughters' heads and declared them daughters of the King, and it was as if I could literally see a garment of confidence clothe the girls.
>
> —Submitted by Cricket

Defining a Man of Integrity

This is one of the most critical aspects in support of a young girl's desire and need for affirmation by the opposite sex at this age. It is vital to paint a portrait of a man of integrity. This will help her choose her male friendships wisely and eventually lead her to select an emotionally and spiritually well-rounded future husband.

I [Doreen] recommend studying Psalm 15 with your daughter to learn the qualities reflected in a man who seeks to live right with God and others. This process also helps your daughter select the man who will impart her blessing if it is to be someone other than her father.

Young women should be made aware of their own vulnerability to attention from the opposite sex. Girls from homes where Dad is absent, distant, or distracted are the most vulnerable. All young women, when they gain an accurate view of what a godly male looks like, can gain the ability to recognize a quality man when she meets one.

> *There is no cosmetic for beauty like happiness.*
>
> —COUNTESS OF BLESSINGTON,
> MARGUERITE GARDINER

When Pam mentors young women, she takes them on the same tour of Scripture she went on to learn how to spot a godly guy. When a teen takes a hard look at the original, she can spot a counterfeit. Josh McDowell teaches youth that "love means to provide and protect." Our girls need to learn what true love looks like.

I [Pam] did a character study of Jesus, the disciples who stayed true to Christ, and Daniel, Joseph, and Boaz to gain a better grasp of what a godly guy might look and act like. It worked. I gave up dating "frogs" and gained a prince of a husband.

If possible, this is also a place where Dad can step in (or another father figure) and share how guys think and how to recognize a good guy. A creative way to do this is to take his daughter into "a man's world" for a day. This will look different for each father. Some dads might take their daughter to a ballpark or a home-building store. If Dad is interested in cars, he could take his daughter to an auto shop or car dealership. Maybe Dad chooses to take his daughter golfing or to a museum. The place and activity is not as important as time together and conversation.

You sir, are supposed to be charming.

—EVER AFTER

As Dad shares and demonstrates how good men provide for and protect those they love, a healthy young woman learns the value of a good man and how to recognize one. Once she learns this important lesson, she can set an example for others.

Stephanie was 16 years old when she attended DOK. Since she was the oldest in this particular group, the younger girls looked to her as a role model. Stephanie already had a steady boyfriend, Nic, and they both were seeking to keep their relationship pure. Five years later, Stephanie and Nic were still virgins on their wedding day. She proudly wore the crown she received at her blessing ceremony on her wedding day.

Today, Stephanie and Nic are youth leaders at their church. Most excitedly for me [Doreen], she has become an MDP facilitator and has carried out the program in her own church as well as several other groups in her community in the last several years. Stephanie's choice to model a healthy romantic relationship continues to positively influence young women around her.

The important lessons you're teaching your daughter now can instill in her the wisdom and confidence she needs to become a woman who makes a difference in the lives of others.

Faith Versus Feelings

For teenage girls gushing with hormones and the accompanying variety of new, exciting, and sometimes scary emotions, one very important topic to present is the difference between feelings and faith. Address the reality that, although they were created with every emotion they have, it does not mean they should always act on them. Teenagers need to see the benefits of self-control and the cause-effect relationship between actions and consequences long before they get to the critical decision points in life.

As adults, we must consider how to express our feelings within our walk of faith. Provide the perspective that God's commandments are for our good and our protection and that obeying them does not kill fun, but brings joy, safety, and contentment to our lives.

Oftentimes, having your daughter meet someone who has overcome a great obstacle is a wonderful way to demonstrate this point. For example: a woman who ended a toxic dating relationship; a woman who had the courage to choose to have her baby in a crisis situation; or a woman who has had a severe illness or disability, yet lives to demonstrate her strong faith in God and live with a spirit of joy. All of these can be examples of women who may have imperfect lives but gave their heart to a perfect Father who redeemed the pain and put them on a path to a future and a hope.

Exposure to college women and successful women leaders who are making good decisions can help a young woman learn by seeing faith walked out in real life. True, personal examples are our best teachers, so if you can create multiple opportunities for your young, developing daughter to be exposed to godly women and hear their stories, she will be enriched.

Her Spiritual Life

Lastly, but certainly not least, cover the importance of your daughter's spiritual relationship with her Heavenly Father. To enable her to focus her thoughts on God, encourage her to journal her prayers (you might purchase or create a pretty journal with a loving note from you expressing your excitement for her in doing this exercise). This will enable your daughter to see how God answers prayer, and she will have documentation in her own writing to go back to in the future when she might become discouraged about another life challenge.

Being able to reflect upon God's faithfulness will help a young woman be faithful to her Heavenly Father, who is faithful to her. Emphasize the value of spending time daily in God's Word (and present the importance of knowing her Heavenly Father through a relationship with Jesus Christ as outlined in Scripture). One of the best ways for your daughter to learn to have a quiet time with Jesus is to have a quiet time with you (another good reason for you to try to be a living example). Have your daughter, or the group of girls, have the same kind of quiet time or devotion time as you do daily.

When you are leading your daughter or group into recognizing their need for a relationship with Jesus Christ, a written covenant helps keep before them the commitment they have made. (In the Appendix, we have provided a simple example. Consider creating a certificate and having it framed so she/they can hang it strategically in their room as a daily reminder.)

Danielle is an example of a young woman whose rite-of-passage experience recharged her spiritual relationship with God:

> I was a very new Christian struggling in my walk with God and didn't even know what God thought about me. I was willing to do anything to get a guy's attention. But no matter how many guys asked for my phone number, chatted me up, or even said they "loved" me, I still hated myself. I resorted to starving myself and cutting in order to physically feel the pain that I was feeling inside.
>
> When I started the DOK and as the weeks went on, I learned more and more about myself and what God thought of me. Today, I know I am a princess and God does have the right prince waiting for me. It was life changing to understand and see myself from God's perspective. Thanks to my rite-of-passage journey, I was able to grow and learn to love God with my whole heart.
> —Danielle

One of today's favorite films for young girls is *The Princess Diaries,* which depicts the transformation of an "ugly duckling" who is awkward and unfinished, into a "beautiful swan," a princess lovely both inside and out. That is whose head you should crown—a princess who has paid the price. It's for this reason that the ground a Modern-Day Princess covers before her rite-of-passage celebration makes the Night of Celebration even more meaningful.

Mentor Moments

One of the main components of my [Pam's] mentoring of young women has always been helping the young woman make critical, vital decisions affecting her purity and dating life.

When Bill and I were youth pastors, we saw that many young women so longed for male attention that they didn't think through or pray through the imperative relationship decisions of life. We developed a Teen Relationship Contract, which is available in contract form online or it is also in *The 10 Best Decisions Every Parent Can Make* (available at www.farrel communications.com). This is a contract teen guys and girls use to help them think through the important elements of a dating relationship, and it includes questions for discussion on topics such as the ones below. (Feel free to use these discussion starters with the young woman in your life.)

- What are the qualities I am looking for in a future mate?
- Do I have those qualities?
- How will my parents know I am mature and responsible enough to date?
- What is a date?
- How do I handle a relationship as it progresses?
- What are God's standards for a physical relationship?
- How do I value and protect my virginity and purity?

When a teen girl thinks through these issues, she moves out of the "at risk" for teen pregnancy group, especially when her parents reward her for her hard work in completing the contract and talk together over her answers. If any answers are of concern to the parent (or mentor; if her parents are unwilling or uninterested in the dialogue), more discussion can be arranged until an agreement can be reached.

Bill and I have always taught, "You make your choices and your choices make you." There are girls waiting for you to choose to invest in their lives! (And some Modern-Day Knights who will be grateful you did! If you are married, perhaps your husband can begin a Raising a Modern-Day Knight group or walk your sons through the *Raising a Modern-Day Knight* material.)

Knights and Princesses build strong, healthy marriages and families, which in turn, build strong, healthy churches and communities. Just as we teach educational skills of math, science, and English; just as we teach life skills such as making your bed, boiling an egg, or washing dishes; we also need to communicate and equip our teens with relationship skills so they can create love lives that last.

The Bible doesn't tell us that Christians will be known for our academics or our ingenuity or our looks, rather it says, "By this all men will know that you are My disciples, if you have love for one another" (John 13:35, NASB).

Teach your daughter or mentee to love and to recognize love. Isn't that what a truly "royal future" is, to love and to be loved? True love—that's the "happily ever after" every girl is looking for.

Mother: The Symphony of Her Life Begins with You

... we cared for you the way a mother cares for her
children. We loved you dearly. Not content to just pass
on the Message, we wanted to give you our hearts. ...

—1 THESSALONIANS 2:7–8 (MSG)

I remember my mother's prayers
and they have always followed me.
They have clung to me all my life.

—ABRAHAM LINCOLN (1809–1865)

A mom is like the orchestra conductor in the symphony of her
daughter's life. Mom, if you tap your baton to the sheet music of
Scripture, some amazing things can happen in your daughter's heart.

Moms have a profound influence on us—for good, or not. Both of
us [Doreen and Pam] feel grateful for positive, proactive mothers who
cared for each of us and influenced our lives in amazing ways, in spite of
their own personal pain or any drama going on in their private lives. Our
mothers' influence gave us a heart for serving others and the confidence
to lead.

Doreen Recalls Thoughts of Her Own Mother

Just the thought of my mother, Ariel, now in her eighties, brings immediate peace to my mind, joy to my heart, and memories that refresh my soul. I am grateful that God's divine plan purposed that I would be raised by a godly mother. I will always associate simple phrases with Mom when I hear them quoted. Things such as:

• Cleanliness is next to godliness.

• Always wear clean underwear. You never know when you'll be in an accident.

• Beauty is in the eye of the beholder.

I carried these and other simple words of wisdom into the lives of my own two daughters and now I'm beginning to see them passed on to my granddaughters. I don't think it's ever been written anywhere that I should have told my girls things like this. It's just the way I heard my mother say certain things repeatedly. We establish traditions by the things we *speak* to the next generation (once again we see the power of our words).

On the other hand, some things are never spoken but rather lived out—modeled daily for us by our mothers. Imprinted upon my mind to this day is a picture of my mom, curled up in her favorite chair, quietly reading God's Word or praying before the rest of the family rose to meet the day.

I did not realize the effect my mother's spiritual discipline had on my life until the early years of my marriage. I chose to attend my first women's Bible study because I was looking to better understand my relationship with the Lord and become a better wife and mother. One particular day at Bible study, the leader began to paint a word picture of a godly woman.

I immediately recognized that many of the attributes and spiritual disciplines creating the masterpiece of a godly woman were those modeled by my very own mother.

I saw clearly, for the first time in my life, that her time spent with God had obviously kept her centered emotionally. Her faith strengthened her trust in God despite many challenges, and she was strong spiritually because of the thousands of mornings spent with her Heavenly Father.

Today, she is abundant in her knowledge of God's Word. She has hidden His Word in her heart (even in her early seventies, she memorized the book of Habakkuk) and the depth of her faith continues to encourage and challenge me as well as others who are a part of her life.

Despite my mother's good qualities, I don't mean to imply that she was, or is, perfect, by any means. But it was her good decisions that made a lasting effect on me. I honestly can't remember very many mistakes my mom made. However, I can clearly remember one.

One particular day, when my sister was 12 and I was 14, we were assigned

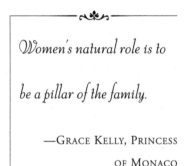

Women's natural role is to be a pillar of the family.

—Grace Kelly, Princess of Monaco

the task of cleaning the pots, pans, and shelves in the lower cabinets of the kitchen. Typical teens, we were both bored within a short time of what seemed to be a major project, so we just lazily moved along knowing Mom was out running errands. To our surprise, she returned much earlier than we expected. When she entered the kitchen and saw our sloppy and unfinished task, in her frustration she took the nearest pan and conked my sister right on the head.

It took my sister by utter surprise because Mom came from behind (and didn't do things like this!). As I watched my mom's unjustified anger turn into shock, and my sister's face turn into a "What just happened?" look, in a nervous response I burst into uncontrollable laughter.

Fortunately, my response broke the tension of the moment and we all ended up laughing together as though we were mimicking a Three Stooges scene. Years later, we discovered in a true confession that Mom had an argument with Dad and was still angry with him when she returned home. When she realized he was gone, her anger exploded on my sister's head. No, moms are not perfect (can you relate?), but moms are called. We are called to be the guardian of the symphony of our daughter's life.

It's Got a Beat I Can Dance To

Some of you might have grown up hearing Dick Clark play songs on *American Bandstand,* then ask for a rating from eager teens. If it was a song with a strong beat, it rated high. My mom [Pam's] would get a high mother rating because she provided a beat for my life I could "dance to." The resounding mantras of my mother's words echo in my heart:
- Take the high road.
- Be part of the solution.
- Be a loyal friend.
- Search for God until you find Him.
- Celebrate all you can in life because life can be traumatic.
- Look for times and ways to mark the moments that matter.

As I look back, I recognize that my mom tried her best to mark my important moments. There were new shoes each Easter and a new backpack with a back-to-school outfit each fall. There were consistent stops at the mom-and-pop store for my favorite Cracker Jack treat after passing a swim test. There was the annual "picture in front of the fireplace" at Christmas and on the front sidewalk the first day of school. She provided a new dress for my first junior-high dance, a dinner party for my Sweet 16th birthday, and a new watch for graduation.

These were small things that added up and built confidence in my heart year after year. Her efforts matched her words that still echo in my heart each day as I rise to lead: "You can do this thing, Pam. Do it well."

My mother is the first to point out her shortcomings, though. She grieves that she came to Christ later in life so she couldn't teach me what she did not know. She regrets she had a tumultuous relationship with my father and felt inadequate to give much relationship advice as I began dating. She wishes that she and her daughters had had a rite-of-passage ceremony. You also might feel inadequate in your motherhood role for some reason, but that's what is so wonderful about God. He takes our best efforts and adds Himself to the mix, in spite of any inadequacies we feel as a parent or any imperfections in our environment.

As the maestro of your daughter's life, what are the main chords God would like you to play in her heart so that someday she can live a life that is a series of beautiful notes? How can you weave in tradition and creativity that will help your daughter sing the song God placed in her heart? The traits your daughter needs to see in you are:

- **S**ecurity
- **I**ndustry
- **N**obility
- **G**enerosity

These are the same traits to begin weaving into her own life so she can live out God's song for her.

Security

To help her sing the song, she needs you, Maestro, to build security in her life. I [Pam] have often wondered how Moses, a man of great courage, obedience, and dedication was such a strong leader when he only had time with his biological mother in his early years.

I sometimes wonder if his sense of security was strong because he knew the story of his mother's sacrifice. She risked her life to simply give birth to her son in a time when all Jewish boys were being murdered. She creatively planned his safety by placing him in a basket in the bulrushes to hide him. She risked her own safety and freedom when she volunteered to be his nurse in the home of the Egyptian princess who discovered him.

This mother's love and sacrifice saved her son's life, enabling him to eventually be greatly used by God. In that same sense, we must be mindful that our choices can influence our daughters' futures. We know that teen girls today face tough decisions. Your daughter needs to feel secure and safe in her relationship with you, Mom. So how can we develop a sense of security or trust in our relationships with our daughters?

First and foremost, I [Doreen] believe there must be the element of trust between mother and daughter. As our daughters begin to develop physically, it generally comes with a growing spirit of independence. Most girls desire to separate in various degrees from the dictates of "mother knows best." They want to try new things and they develop a more adventurous spirit.

Peer pressure often adds to this new spirit of wanting to see and try things differently than what has been the norm at home. I am talking about small things—like the way they dress, speak, comb their hair, and so on. I am not referring to choices that endanger their lives physically, mentally, emotionally, or spiritually.

A wise and understanding mother will not consider this move toward independence as a threat. She will see it as an opportunity to guide her daughter through the steps of developing wisdom in her decision-making process. Even though, at this present time, your daughter may not have yet developed skill at making good decisions, be encouraged, Mom! God's Word promises that His Word and those you have spoken into her life will not have fallen on deaf ears, even though it might feel or appear like it right now (Isaiah 55:11).

This might be an opportunity to increase your measure of faith and trust God in a greater way because there will be moments when fear will want to overwhelm you. Take courage: The Lord your God is with you. Remember, "He answered their prayers because they trusted in him" (1 Chronicles 5:20b).

Demonstrating your trust in your daughter is the greatest gift you can give her at this stage of her life. Allow her to begin making decisions about relatively small things that may be different from the choices you would make for her. Ask her first to present the alternatives with their pros and cons. Then ask her to explain her decision and the reasoning behind it.

As she begins to demonstrate skill at this level of decision-making, gradually increase the importance of the decisions you allow her to make, sharing your perspective and recommendations when she asks for them. This will be hard, especially at first, but it will prove excellent in building your relationship!

Let me emphasize that there will be times, of course, when you must stand firm for what you know protects her integrity or her future. We, as mothers, are one of her God-given authorities and she must understand that, at times, you prove your love by saying "No." God will hold us accountable for the manner in which we do that.

Mary is a biblical example of a young woman who made good decisions. When she was at a critical moment of her life (after the angel came to her and announced she would be mother to the Savior), she was wise enough to seek out a mentor, her cousin Elizabeth. You might want to brainstorm with your daughter all the women in the Bible and what wise decisions they made. Then shift the conversation to choices you are glad you made as a young woman, and the choices that lie before your daughter on the journey ahead.

Often at this age, if Mom thinks something is good (such as a rite of passage) but there isn't enough evidence to prove it to her daughter, it becomes a questionable matter in the young girl's mind. Because of our American culture, most young girls are not familiar with the term "rite of passage" and they do not have an understanding of what it entails. Therefore, there might be a certain hesitancy to embrace the concept wholeheartedly.

However, as you share about this journey, the thought will likely come to her that hopefully, some of her friends may wish to participate and she might consider the possibility of meeting new ones. (If you are a mom or if you are a mentor who is planning to have a group, keep this in mind.) I [Doreen] have not yet found a girl who does not want to experience the joy of being crowned with a tiara and having her father, or another significant man, publicly affirm her, whether it is just with family in the living room, or in a church or community center filled with people.

If your daughter is hesitant to participate in a mother/daughter rite of passage or to join a group, don't be discouraged. Understand that forcing the issue will never provide good results. Remember, patience and your daughter's personality are both important factors in creating an invi-

> *A mother is one to whom you hurry when you are troubled.*
>
> —EMILY DICKINSON

tation that she will more readily accept. Consider starting some small traditions to prepare the path.

As a facilitator, I [Doreen] preface the following story with the fact that this mom was as determined for her daughter to attend as her daughter was not. Clare called several times requesting prayer, even at 10 o'clock after the parents' meeting, quite distraught over her daughter's unwillingness to attend. Here is her story in her own words:

Several weeks before our church was scheduled to host an MDP weekend, I had been thinking that our oldest daughter, Sarah, ought to attend. She had been quite angry with us for several months due to my husband's job change that prompted our family's move. This left her feeling the loss of good friends and facing the reality that she would have to work at making new ones. She had angrily exclaimed one day that she hated us for doing that to her.

As a modern teenager, she constantly exuded the know-it-all attitude. Therefore, when I mentioned attending the weekend retreat to her, my hopes took a nose-dive as she callously replied that she did not see that there was anything she could learn from it.

When I mentioned Sarah's reply to my husband he announced, "With an attitude like that, this retreat might be just what she needs." As we started making plans to convince her, I prayed desperately for God to change her will.

At the parents' meeting a few days prior to the weekend, I mentioned to Doreen how reluctant she was about the idea. Doreen listened patiently then offered her standard escape clause that she presents at every first session to all the girls:

"How many of you are here because your mom wanted you to come? [Often most hands are raised.] I want you to be here because YOU want to be here. If after the first session, you believe that this class is not for you, I will be your advocate and I will personally go to your parents and explain to them this is not the time for you to attend the class, no questions asked."

She then told me that to date, there has never been one girl, in the hundreds she's taken through the program, who has left and requested Doreen to speak to her parents.

So armed, we dragged Sarah to the first meeting that turned out to be a fun-filled night of makeovers and manners with friendly girls close to her own age. After the evening concluded and we drove home, she decided not to drop out.

At the closing ceremony, one of the other mothers said, "One of the great beauties of this program is that it really reinforces all the teaching we have been giving our children at home." A few weeks later my own experience bore this out.

Sarah told me about the Man of Integrity class that highlights the importance of abstinence. My ears perked up. For years my husband and I had been teaching our children the value of saving themselves for marriage, but I often wondered how much was getting through. Then Sarah told me what they learned about STDs and how easily they could be caught and spread.

She said, "You know, Mom, I think sleeping around with a whole bunch of people is disgusting. I never want to do anything like that!" Imagine my enormous relief.

There have been other benefits, too. Seeing my husband publicly bless our daughter was priceless. Since then my husband's eyes have been opened to his power to bless us through his speech. I have noticed him more eager to "give praise when praise is due."

—Clare T.

Industry

Being a mom, you KNOW how much work life takes. Your daughter needs you to model and build into her a strong work ethic. Take a look at Proverbs 31 and note all the verbs in this passage about the virtuous woman:

- She *brings* him good, not harm, all the days of her life.
- She *selects* wool and flax and *works* with eager hands.
- She is like the merchant ships, *bringing* her food from afar.
- She *gets up* while it is still dark; she *provides* food for her family and portions for her servant girls.
- She *considers* a field and *buys* it; out of her earnings she *plants* a vineyard.
- She *sets* about her work vigorously; her arms are strong for her tasks.
- She *sees* that her trading is profitable, and her lamp *does not go out* at night.
- In her hand she *holds* the distaff and *grasps* the spindle with her fingers.
- She *opens* her arms to the poor and *extends* her hands to the needy. . . .
- She *makes* coverings for her bed; she *is clothed* in fine linen and purple. . . .
- She *makes* linen garments and *sells* them, and *supplies* the merchants with sashes.
- She *is clothed* with strength and dignity; she *can laugh* at the days to come.
- She *speaks* with wisdom, and faithful instruction is on her tongue.
- She *watches* over the affairs of her household and does not eat the bread of idleness. (Proverbs 31:12–27, emphasis added)

Reward her hard work as creatively as you can. Author Nancy Sebastian Meyer gave her budding teen a challenge and a reward that marked her entry into the teen years in grand style. Nancy explains the adventure:

Just before Becky turned 12, our youth pastors invited parents to a meeting where they gave us some great ideas on helping teens transition into their adult role. One of those was the 13-coming-of-age celebration. We put our own twist on "bat mitzvah."

For Becky's 12th birthday, Rich and I gave her a carefully prepared notebook of 12 challenges: 3 spiritual, 3 physical, 3 mental, and 3 practical. The idea was to give her a year (with help, support, and accountability) to tackle some really hard growth-oriented tasks that would—by her 13th birthday—give her victories on which she could enter the turbulent teen years. We were proactively setting her up for success!

For example, one of the three physical challenges was to get her gym teacher to sign off on how fast she should be able to run a mile at this age, and then accomplish that target by her 13th birthday.

An example of a practical challenge was the "Been-There-Done-That List": 12 ordinary tasks every teen should be able to do, such as change a lightbulb, do the family laundry for a week, change the oil in the car, and more. Then, to celebrate the actual entry to her teens on her 13th birthday, we invented the "Teen Triumph."

We rented our church's fellowship hall and hired the church chef to create a dessert smorgasbord the Sunday afternoon closest to Becky's birthday. We invited all of the significant and influential people in her life—family, friends, teachers, coaches—and asked them not to bring presents or a card, but bring "a book that should be in everyone's library" and write a special message in the front to Becky honoring her birthday and her character.

As people arrived, they could look over a few display tables of the many things from Becky's life that showed her accomplishments (a bowling trophy), hobbies (an American Girl doll), talents (her viola), interests (a book on sea life), and so on.

We began with a prayer of thankfulness and explained that we would begin with dessert and an open mic for everyone to share their stories about Becky (we taped the entire event). This was followed by a formal program where Rich and I shared and celebrated Becky's various challenges with everyone and gave her gifts in keeping with the four areas of achievement (The Library of Love—the books each family/individual gave as a gift—was the Mental Challenge reward).[1]

[Note: More on this type of entry into the teen world and specifics on how to create a personalized challenge can be found in *Suddenly They're 13* by Dave and Claudia Arp.]

Nobility

Your daughter needs to see you as a woman who respects herself, and she needs to learn how to have self-respect so she can value herself as God values her. In a world fraught with pressure and societal expectations, it can be a challenge to help a young lady see herself from God's vantage point and make choices that reflect that viewpoint.

Often, mothers do not agree with some of the choices their daughters make, such as the way they wear their hair, or the shoes, clothes, or jewelry they choose to wear. Most every mom, at some point in this season of her daughter's life, will have to bite her lip and say, "It's your choice!" All along you will have to fight those thoughts that you would prefer not to be seen with her because the tails of her eyeliner have just met her temples, her clothes look like they came from Aardvark's, or her favorite shoes just added a foot to her height now causing her to tower over you!

I [Doreen] believe the defining complementary differences between trust and respect are these:

You demonstrate trust by *verbalizing* your encouragement and challenging your daughter to make her own healthy choices.

You show your respect for her by *remaining silent* when she makes choices you might not agree with and you allow her to experience the consequences, either good or bad, accordingly. This will take some discernment on your part. While you have been entrusted by God to protect and nurture your daughter, there will be times she needs to make her own decisions.

There may also be times you must confront her unhealthy behaviors or choices. Pray for wisdom in this area. If necessary, seek advice from other women you trust and respect. A good lesson to remember regarding your daughter is to choose your battles wisely.

Mom, as you prepare for her rite of passage, keep in mind that instilling nobility in your daughter also requires addressing her sexual purity. Generations X and Y have been equipped with many wonderful books, seminars, and DVDs on this subject for teenage girls and their parents.

My personal recommendation is that you establish some quality time to be spent taking advantage of one of these resources *before* you begin the rite of passage. Or you can include it in your one-on-one time with your daughter. Consider how the information will be presented because it is personal and private and success will depend on your own and your daughter's comfort level (keeping in mind that it is sometimes necessary to move beyond comfort to address what is important).

You may feel that this is an area where you've made unhealthy choices and so feel hesitant to give advice. But your instruction and encouragement are still blessings to your daughter, Mom. And remember, too, her time spent with a mentor and/or other girls who practice abstinence will validate and confirm the importance of her choice to be sexually pure or to stay chaste until marriage from this point on. God truly has blessed both of these commitments. He honors righteous living and a repentant heart.

You have heard several examples of how a rite of passage helps prevent girls from making unwise choices. It also helps a girl restart in this vital area:

The hardest week for me in my rite of passage was when we addressed "The Men in Our Lives and Sexual Purity" because I was the only girl in the class who had not saved herself for marriage. I felt worthless and ashamed and that God would never forgive me for the things I had done.

Going through the class, I learned that God is not only a very loving God but He is also very merciful. We were taught some of the greatest lessons a teenager could learn, one of which was how to turn our pain into power. I may not have felt like a daughter of the King when I started the class, but through the course God moved in my life and healed my heart.

When I walked down the aisle to meet my father, I knew boldly that I was a daughter of the King. I was lost but He (God) found me and carried me to redemption. Being a part of Daughters of the King has changed my life forever.

—Lani

We are blessed to serve a God who redeems our brokenness. As your daughter begins to see herself as a daughter of the King, talk freely about forgiveness and the importance of making the choice, regardless of past mistakes, to move forward with a determination to view her sexuality as a precious gift, meant only to be shared with the future husband God has for her.

Generosity

One of my [Pam's] favorite women in the Bible has only a few sentences written about her, but they speak volumes about her generous heart:

> A woman named Lydia, from the city of Thyatira, a seller of purple fabrics, a worshiper of God, was listening; and the Lord opened her heart to respond to the things spoken by Paul. And when she and her household had been baptized, she urged us, saying, "If you have judged me to be faithful to the Lord, come into my house and stay." And she prevailed upon us. (Acts 16:14–15, NASB)

Immediately after her conversion to the Lord, she wanted to give. Equip your daughter to be generous and kind. One way of doing this is by your own example. Are you generous? Generosity doesn't automatically mean monetary gifts, though that can be a blessing to others.

You can be generous with your time. When a friend needs someone to listen to her or support her through a life circumstance, do you make time to be the friend she needs? If there's a family you know that's going through a difficult time, do you use your time and resources to take them a meal or send them a note of encouragement? Do you give to missions or charity organizations? Even if you give a small amount, caring for the less fortunate teaches your daughter that helping others—even in different countries—should be a priority to her. Both small and large gifts can be a blessing to others—and to your daughter.

The passing of gifts is a wonderful way to mark a rite of passage into womanhood. These gifts can mark the moments that matter, such as entering womanhood at menses; entrance to high school, dating, or driving; graduation from high school, college, or graduate school; or upon her engagement and her wedding. The celebration of a rite-of-passage ceremony is one more opportunity to pass on family values with a family gift.

Author Eva Marie Everson writes this of her family:

We are a family of mother/daughter gifts! I wear my grandmother's engagement ring (my mother had it before me), and my daughter Jessica already has my grandmother's cocktail ring. I have a cameo ring with 1910 engraved in it that was given to my mother by my grandfather and then given to me on my 18th birthday. Jessica, when she marries, will receive my great-grandmother's wedding ring (which is her great-great-grandmother's ring).

There are handmade quilts and bed throws (one made of tobacco twine by my great-grandmother for her daughter—my grandmother—and then given to her daughter, my mother) that I will be given one day. My mother has her grandmother's wedding china, her mother's wedding china, and her own wedding china!

My grandmother wore a long strand of pearls. It was so long my mother had it cut in half. She has half and I have half. When my mother gifted me with it she wrote on a card: "These pearls were worn by a great lady. Wear them as a great lady would."[2]

If you choose to incorporate gift-giving in your daughter's rite of passage, ask yourself what you have that might be able to serve as the new symbol for all future women entering womanhood in coming generations in your family. One enterprising mother redeemed a negative situation when she had her wedding ring from a failed marriage melted down and turned into a necklace that was to be passed from mother to daughter for future generations. Another mother took her grandmother's jewelry and asked her artsy friend to create something new from the old pieces that she gave her daughter.

> *If any one faculty of our nature may be called more wonderful than the rest, I do think it is memory.*
>
> —JANE AUSTEN

Mom, What's in the Symphony Program?

Presently, you have the high calling to be a role model to your teenage daughter, with a desire to create a bond that will last a lifetime. Because you are reading this book, we're sure you are a proactive mom seeking to be in tune to what your daughter faces on a daily basis. But what is in store for you in the coming years? A current mentor to girls in this generation is Angela Thomas, who wrote an article giving some pointers on the stages of a teen girl's life:[3]

What You Can Expect: Ages 11–14

You've suddenly become the most annoying person on the face of the earth and have no idea what you're talking about most of the time; at least that's how she perceives you today. Tomorrow may be totally different.

She lives in a world that tells her to be more grown-up and sophisticated than she's ready for. Keep a close watch on who and what is influencing her choices.

What You Can Expect: Ages 15–16

This is the fun stage of your daughter's life. She's become more confident, and her talents and areas of interest are narrowing down.

Here are a few tips to help you stay connected with her:

- Step into her world and find out what she loves. She may have totally different interests than you.
- Don't try to make her into a carbon copy of yourself or another sibling. She's one-of-a-kind.
- Get to know her. Tap into her personality and discover what motivates her.
- Encourage her to seek God's plan for her life.
- Keep in mind your teen daughter is still a teenager, not yet an adult.

What You Can Expect: Ages 17–19

She needs your guidance now more than your lectures.

She wants you to talk to her, not at her. She wants your input but needs to make her own decisions.

⚜

You might be right in the middle of these years, or you might be feeling a bit overwhelmed now knowing what's to come. We've said it before, this will take courage, Mom, but you can do it. One of the skills I [Pam] teach parents when raising a teen (and especially when dealing with a prodigal child) is to parent "by faith and not fear." This same advice is well suited for the mentor to apply as well. It is always better to influence from a place of faith—not fear.

Fear says, "Don't get pregnant before you are married."

Faith says, "I know you will make wise relationship choices."

Fear says, "Don't drive drunk! Don't do drugs!"

Faith says, "I know I will hear a great report about you from the parents and leaders when I see them tomorrow."

Fear says, "You can't go if I can't be there with you."

Faith says, "I see that you have checked to see responsible adults are there to supervise, and you make great choices in friends. Have a wonderful time reflecting God's love to others as you go."

Fear says to a daughter, "I don't trust you." This makes her think, *My parents already think I'm going to do it, so I will try it.* (Whatever sin "it" is.)

Faith says just the opposite, "I trust you. I trust that you will honor God. I trust that you will honor our family. I trust that you will honor your friendship circle. I trust you will honor all your leaders who have poured their time and talent into your life. I trust you will honor yourself and your inner core values."

Trust builds a desire to obey, to achieve, to excel, to accomplish all that God has for her. This isn't to say that she won't make mistakes along the way, of course. Or that you won't have to practice discernment. But part of the growing process (for all of us) is learning from our mistakes. And as she grows, your trust and faith in her will instill the confidence she needs to become the woman God wants her to be.

There will be times when you might feel as though finding common ground with your daughter is impossible. You are not alone, Mom! Your daughter's tween and teen years can be challenging for her *and* you. The key is to consistently be a source of love, trust, and truth for her. Author

Linda Newton knows the challenges of raising a strong-willed teen daughter, who is a bit "myopic" like every teen. Linda writes:

When my firstborn, Sarah, turned 14, a new era of parenting dawned. Suddenly the parents that she had once loved and respected became "so lame," by her definition. She decided that she could handle herself without our input and we were unfair with all of our strict rules. Convinced she was held to a higher standard, the last line of her lament would be, "It's just because I'm a pastor's kid." Then she would roll her eyes, flip her long blond hair behind her shoulder, and flounce to her room.

That's when I returned to Dr. Dobson's Web site and his book *Parenting Isn't for Cowards,* desperate for more instructions on surviving these turbulent teen years. One afternoon, shortly after my daughter's nineteenth birthday, as I was staining trim for our new home, Sarah walked into the garage with a two-year-old in tow.

"Well, who do we have here?" I asked, leaning down to make eye contact with a beautiful blue-eyed boy holding Sarah's hand.

"His name is Eric," Sarah informed me. "His mom is in my photography class at college. She likes my work and she wanted me to take his picture, so I brought him here to take advantage of our view. It's no use talking to him, Mom. Eric doesn't talk. His mother doesn't spend enough time with him. When I have my kids, I'm going to quit my job and stay home with them like you. I'm going to talk to them about the flowers, trees, and God. I'm going to do it just like you did."

I couldn't believe my ears. My first thought was, *Where's the mother ship and what have you done with Sarah?!* My once recalcitrant daughter continued to tout her plans to parent like me. I continued to stain trim as I listened to her, afraid if I stopped and looked her in the eye, she might realize what she was actually saying. It turns out Dr. Dobson was right again. At 19, Sarah returned to the dimpled darling I once knew.

While she'd called me lame, unfair, and old-fashioned, that day in the garage, I finally heard her in so many words rise up and call me blessed. And I believe I earned it![4]

As moms of teens, one goal is to move a teen from a self-centered view to an others-centered view. Within a few more years, Linda received a vivid picture of the fruit of her labors in this endeavor. Linda writes:

As I sat in the Denver airport, on my way to speak at a retreat in Oklahoma, my cell phone rang. It was my husband, Bruce. "Sarah has her commissioning ceremony for the Air Force on Monday and she wants us to go," he informed me.

"What?" I was caught off guard. My oldest daughter, Sarah, was born fiercely independent. At 28 years old, in the middle of her doctorate in psychology, she began talking to us about her desire to help the folks coming back from Iraq with Post Traumatic Stress Disorder. Her husband, Shaun, was all for it. Shaun had served two terms in Iraq before he became an EMT. He was even considering re-enlisting to join his wife in the Air Force.

Well, I'm glad he's supportive, but I'm not convinced that my five-foot-two, blue-eyed blond daughter will be all right in the military while our country is at war! I said to myself again and again.

I worried about where she would be stationed. In conversations about her enlisting, she assured us that the nature of her work would keep her out of harm's way. But I know my daughter. She was the little girl on the swing set always yelling, "Push me higher, Mommy. I a big girl!"

I hadn't shared my many concerns with her. I never wanted to be a neurotic or meddling mother. She felt like the Lord wanted her to help soldiers and who was I to get in her way?

I'm her Mama. That's who! I thought, sitting in the airport. And as Erma Bombeck said: "Those stretch marks don't tan." She owes me after all she put me through! It became very clear in that moment that I was not okay with my petite, beautiful girl becoming an officer in the United States Air Force during wartime.

Lord, this is too tough for me. I need Your help to deal with this—now! I felt instant peace but no resolve as I prayed.

After my talk during the Saturday evening session, I placed a chair in the middle of the room and invited women who needed prayer to come up. After hours of praying for God's healing touch for His daughters, one of the women volunteered, "I think we should pray for Linda."

"I'll never turn down prayer," I responded immediately, asking the group to pray for my daughter. "I have to confess that I am not crazy about her idea to enlist," I opened up to the group. Then Ami, the senior pastor's wife, prayed a passionate prayer that God would give me a revelation or a sign that would calm my fears for Sarah.

Bright and early Monday morning, Bruce and I picked up Sarah and Shaun and headed four hours north for Sarah's commissioning ceremony.

When every uniformed person in the building gathered to watch my daughter stand beside the American flag as she was sworn in as a Second Lieutenant in the United States Air Force, I had to fight back tears.

After a lunch spent discussing future plans, we started for home. About an hour down the road, we passed a green sedan driving on the shoulder of the road. "Slow down and I'll get the license and report it to the CHP," Shaun urged.

As we did, we noticed the driver, an older man, seemed unaware that he was driving illegally. Just as we moved out of his way, he swerved onto the highway, weaving in and out of lanes. Before we could blink, he had clipped a white pickup about four car lengths ahead of us. We watched in what seemed to be slow motion as the truck slammed against the guardrail—dust and car parts flying everywhere.

We pulled over to the side of the road as Bruce immediately dialed 911. Then Sarah, who was sitting in the backseat beside me, leaned forward, tapped her husband on the shoulder, and said, "Are we ready, Babe? Are we ready?" I was thinking, *Ready? Ready for what? We're on a freeway in the fast lane.* But before I could ask my question, Sarah and Shaun had jumped out of the car and into oncoming traffic.

In what felt like slow motion, I watched my diminutive daughter's blond ponytail swinging in the wind as she flagged down an 18-wheeler to tell the driver about the accident ahead. I then jumped out of the car and followed her to the crushed pickup. Shaun was already tending to a three-year-old in the front seat with a cut on her cheek. All the while Sarah was calming down the driver. Speaking half English and half Spanish, she asked the woman for her cell phone and called the lady's brother to tell him where she was.

A CHP desk officer from the station close by the freeway had spotted the commotion and came to the scene. He seemed to have no problem deferring to Sarah, who was instructing everyone around what to do.

"Do you have a first-aid kit?" Sarah asked him. He handed her the kit, and she pointed to the driver of the green sedan and told the officer, "You need to get that man's keys. I think he might be demented. He doesn't need to be on the road." The officer responded to Sarah's instructions immediately.

Grabbing the officer's first-aid kit with confidence, Sarah riffled through it searching for the things she needed to make the woman more comfortable as she kept assuring her that the ambulance would arrive soon.

I realized in that moment that I was absolutely useless except to pray, so I moved against the guardrail to get out of everyone's way. As I did, I heard God's still small voice speak so clearly in my mind: Your daughter is not a little girl anymore, Linda. She is a grown woman capable of helping people. You have to let her go so that she can do that.[5]

Every parent wants to see his or her child reach her full potential—and that starts now, Mom. Remember the simple acrostic SING and soon you will enjoy seeing your daughter dance to the song God placed into her heart and into the bright future He has for her.

Who's in the Choir?

Since we're talking about singing, now is a good time to point out that it takes many voices to move a young woman forward in her life; her mom, her dad, and her mentors create a choir of wisdom that surround her life and help her sing the song God intended for her. Let's take a closer look at mentor/mom relationships, shall we?

Both of my [Doreen's] daughters, during their teenage years, were fraught with the highest highs and the lowest of lows emotionally, as is true of most teenage girls. I am grateful for the mentors God placed in their lives during these "peaks and valleys." I was also grateful mentors were there on ordinary days as well.

One day when my younger daughter, Kamy, was in junior high, she told me about an essay she had been assigned to write. It was to be about the person she most respected in her life. I must confess, I wanted her to choose me. (On the inside I felt like the donkey in *Shrek* as he jumps up and down crying out to Shrek, "Pick me! Pick me!" At times, I feel that way even today!) I was trying to keep this particular desire of my heart in check so I offered to help her make a list of various individuals she respected. After several minutes she announced confidently that she would write about Alane.

Alane was one of Kamy's youth leaders at church. I knew that Alane was an excellent choice because she had been obviously investing herself in my daughter's life. Alane was, and is, a great listener. She loved to study and teach God's Word and was content to be single. She did not rush into or open doors to unhealthy male relationships. She was a great influence on Kamy. It took no time at all for Kamy to write a thoughtful paper about Alane and she ultimately received an A on her essay.

Then, several years later, Kamy arrived home one day from high school. I was sitting at the dining-room table addressing Christmas cards. As she headed for the refrigerator, she tossed a paper on the table and said, "Read it, Mom. I got an A on it." To my surprise the title of the essay was "The Person I Admire Most in My Life—My Mom."

I wept as I read the loving tribute Kamy had given to me. As she sat down at the table with me, I listened to her tell me that she had discussed with Alane about whom she should write. I gained a very important insight that day: *A mentor is often a mother's best advocate!*

At times a mentor will confirm things that you have said numerous times to that precious young girl of yours, but which have not previously sunk in! She'll return home and share her new revelation with *you*! Oh, those moments when we mothers must join in our children's enthusiasm and rejoice that they had such an epiphany without saying a word or rolling our eyes!

Sometimes a mentoring relationship will be short-lived, but that does not negate the power or impact it will have on your daughter, you, and her mentor. I [Doreen] have found myself in the role of short-term mentor to hundreds of teenage girls over the past decade. I have taken great joy in helping them discover their God-given gifts and enabling them to see their value in God's eyes. I have enjoyed many other wonderful opportunities to see Him working in their lives, and I have frequently been able to become an advocate for their mothers.

As I've [Pam] seen numerous times, a mom and a mentor can be a powerful team in encouraging a young woman to discover her God-given potential. I'm going to speak directly to mentors for a moment.

Team Up by Giving Honor: Give respect and the benefit of the doubt to each other. Teen girls can be a little dramatic. It is likely Mom isn't nearly the monster a daughter might whine she is to her group. In the same way, a mentor might not be the taskmaster a mentee might make her out to be. If you are concerned over something a young woman might claim to have happened, I have found it strategic to say, "This sounds important. I will go with you to talk to your (mom or mentor) so you can talk this out with her." If it is hyperbole, the young woman may backpedal her opinion quickly.

I find it important to say to the girl, especially those with moms who might have growth issues in their own lives, "I am sure your mom loves you. God gave you your mom to help you be all that He has planned for you. No one is perfect. Why don't we create a plan to help you _____ (fill in the blank with the perceived need from the girl's point of view)? Try loving your mom through God's power. Obey your mom with God's grace. Respect and trust your mom as an expression of trust in God."

The Bible reminds us to "be devoted to one another in [sisterly] love. Honor one another above yourselves" (Romans 12:10). Your mentee will feel safer and more willing to trust you and her mother if she senses mutual respect and admiration between the two of you.

Team Up by Giving Friendship: Okay, Mom, this section is for you, too. You may or may not initially be best friends with your daughter's mentor. If you attend a large church, her youth leader, her Bible study leader, an older young woman from the college group, or the youth pastor's wife might be a wonderful mentor, but you might not know her very well. Reach out and build a relationship with her.

Whether you're the mom or the mentor, you can keep confidences your daughter or mentee might have shared, but you can still share hopes, dreams, and opinions that concern the daughter/mentee. It is thoughtful for Mom and mentor to get to know each other since you are playing such vital roles in the young woman's life.

The moms of my mentees have done some amazingly kind things for me: brought over casseroles, dropped a note of thanks in the mail with gift cards for coffee, given a gift card for a restaurant date with my husband, or provided movie tickets to thank me for the extra time I had spent with her daughter. In the same way, I try to remember the mom's birthday or send my own notes of thanks. Ephesians 4:3 encourages us to "make every effort to keep the unity of the Spirit through the bond of peace."

The daughter/mentee will capture much wisdom for her life by watching you both use kindness and empathy to build a strong relationship with one another.

Team Up with Prayer: One of the most powerful tools for growth in anyone's life is to be prayed for. Mom, consider going through the same devotional, using the same prayer promise book, or forging through the same Bible study so that you will be privately traversing the same territory, and praying the same things for your daughter and her mentor. (By doing this on your own, you never have to make her feel "double-teamed," as if she is being hit from two sides.)

However, feel free to pray, all three of you—mom, mentor, and daughter—trusting God together for the growth, wisdom, and strength that every young woman needs in order to forge a fantastic foundation for life and love. James 5:16b (NASB) promises, "The effective prayer of a righteous [wo]man can accomplish much." Your daughter/mentee will feel loved and valued as she sees you both spend your precious time on her behalf. Mentoring pays off; it produces women who are leaders now and will be in the future.

It takes a choir around a soloist to really highlight her voice; in the same way, loving adults surrounding a Modern-Day Princess will make her life SING!

Mentor Moment

I [Pam] mentored daughter and mom, Karly and Debe, at the same time in different settings over several years. Mom, Debe, was the first woman I mentored as a senior pastor's wife, and she went on to be a part of our ministry staff for over 15 years. Debe explains our relationship below:

As our children enter the teenage years, life seems to get more complicated . . . for the whole family! I'm a mother of four kids and three of them are girls. From as young as 12 years old, their lives began to get "bigger." When the hormones started changing, so did their emotions. It seemed they got bigger too! Because relationships are so important to girls, friendships are what they value most in life.

It's during these pre-teen and teenage years that many girls begin spending more time with friends and less time with family. For a number of reasons, girls often feel uncomfortable talking to their mothers about certain things. In fact, some of their challenges probably include their relationships with their moms! But what do they do with questions that their friends can't answer? Who do they turn to next?

It is my conviction that our teenage children need mentors; but not just anyone. As I mentioned, relationships are so valuable to girls; a mentor for my daughters needed to be someone they could trust.

When Pam chose to mentor my daughter Karly, I was

thrilled. Pam had been a mentor in my own life, as well as a dear friend. I respected and loved her. She had many of the characteristics any mom would want to see in her daughter. Karly's and Pam's personalities were very similar, which contributed to the compatibility they shared. They were both driven, evangelistic, creative, outgoing, and held high standards of integrity.

In fact, they looked alike! Most people assumed Pam was her mother! You might think that would have bothered me. I decided that if she was going to look like someone other than me, I was glad it was Pam. I attributed much of that similarity to God's presence that clearly came through both of them. (Not to mention, it was hard to deny the truth. Pam and Karly both had blond hair, fair skin, athletic "dancer's bodies," and enjoyed being "up front." But I'm short, have dark hair, olive skin, there's definitely not an athletic bone in my body, and I prefer being behind the scenes.)

Karly and I enjoyed a very close mother/daughter relationship throughout her teen years. Even so, I knew that a mentoring relationship would greatly benefit her personal and spiritual growth. Karly wanted to step out in ministry and she needed a courageous, experienced leader to guide her in a way that I couldn't have.

One of Pam's strengths is to motivate others to live beyond "average." She had big dreams and lots of ideas for obtaining those. But most of all, she had great trust in a big God who could make all things possible. I think that kids often think their moms have to say encouraging things to them because that's what moms do. But when someone other than their mom believes in them . . . wow!

Pam and Karly's mentoring relationship began in very casual settings. Pam was a young mom with three small boys. Karly was at the perfect age for babysitting and helping with household chores. It was a win-win situation. Some of their most meaningful conversations took place while folding clothes together. It's amazing to think that Karly is now a young mom with three young children.

In all honesty, it's easy for moms to feel hurt or get jealous when our daughters are seeking the advice and guidance of another woman. It's common to have thoughts like, *Why does she need someone else in her life . . . besides me?* That's where I felt especially blessed. It was that trust factor.

I never worried about what Karly might tell Pam about me or what things Pam might say in response. I knew that whatever it was, positive or negative, it was spoken in love. I was secure with my relationship with both Karly and Pam.

I must admit, at first it was difficult when Karly would come home, excited to share something Pam had said to her. I would think to myself, *I've already told you the same thing! Why are you acting like Pam helped you discover something I've already explained to you?* But after thinking about it a little more, I realized the beauty in it all. Does it really matter which voice got through to her as long as she got the message? And furthermore, I appreciated that God used someone in her life and in mine to accomplish that! I realized that Pam and I were part of a team!

If I knew that Karly was facing something difficult in her life and needed extra support, I knew I could call on Pam. I could count on her to pray, make a phone call, or spend time with her. It helped so much to know there was a godly woman I could turn to when I felt overwhelmed or inadequate to say or do the right things. Other times it was for confirmation that I was on the right track after all.

I believe that by trusting Pam and sharing my daughter with Pam, she, too, has been blessed. They share a very special relationship. Today Karly is married, mom to three, and mentors girls through music and drama ministry. She considers Pam "her second mom." They still look and act alike and I am still okay with that! I look at it this way: What mom wouldn't want her daughter to look and act like a woman of character and influence?[6]

Even though I [Pam] mentored Karly and Debe, I learned so much from Debe about what a healthy mother looks and acts like when another woman is mentoring her child. This example helped me look for, encourage, then applaud my own children's mentors and not feel jealous when my kids built strong relationships with godly leaders. If you guard against envy and keep your child's future in sight, mentoring can be a blessing to both you *and* your daughter.

6

Mentors: Influencing the Next Generation

. . . teach the older women to lead a holy life.
They must not tell lies about others. They must not
let wine control them. Instead, they must teach what
is good. Then they can train the younger women.

—TITUS 2:3–4A (NIRV)

The glory of friendship is not the outstretched hand, nor
the kindly smile, nor the joy of companionship; it is the
spiritual inspiration that comes to one when you discover
that someone else believes in you and is willing to trust you.

—RALPH WALDO EMERSON

A woman is walking along the beach. She sees an older woman picking up starfish and tossing them into the sea. The young woman, thinking the older woman's efforts futile, asks, "Why do you do that? There are so many starfish, and the sea's waves unceasingly beat up against the shore. You toss a few back, but what difference does it make?"

The older woman picks up a starfish, flings it into the ocean, and says, "It made a difference to that one!"[1]

In the preface of my [Pam's] book *Woman of Influence,* I write:

Measuring the full impact of influence is nearly impossible. When I was a little girl, I loved to pick the dandelions when they were fluffy and white. I'd blow, and hundreds of little helicopters would fly into the air. I tried to watch where they all went, but as they got caught in the breeze, many would blow higher and higher until they disappeared. Just like those seeds, influence often isn't noticed until it blossoms later in the garden of someone else's life. Our words and actions may land close to home, or they may be carried far and wide.[2]

The thrill of mentoring is that you never know how far your influence may go in another young woman's life. You might mentor the next president, missionary, director of women's ministry, best-selling author, or the woman who discovers the cure for cancer or HIV! You might also be mentoring a host of wonderful future moms, wives, and community, business, and church leaders. Your influence matters.

As you read the stories we will share with you in this section, consider the qualities learned from each mentor. Are you modeling these qualities for your daughter or mentee? Are there areas in your life that need improvement?

Doreen's Mentors

For more than 35 years I have had the privilege of having several mentors, women who have significantly impacted my life. Some I didn't initially recognize as "mentors" but in hindsight I clearly have seen their mentoring touch. Others were purposely chosen because I sought to gain their wisdom and attain the knowledge to live as well as they did.

In my early years of marriage and living two thousand miles away from my mother for the first time, the Lord gave me a wonderful friend and mentor in Emilie.

We came to know each other through working together for a local dentist. I was immediately intrigued by her because she was born with a birth defect. She only had the full use of her little finger and thumb on both hands. The other three fingers were stunted at the knuckle. One particular day over lunch she told me how she had applied to dental school, and her future professor said she would never make it through dental school because of her deformity. Through sheer determination, she graduated at the top of her class and became an excellent hygienist.

More amazed, I discovered that she also played the piano, typed, and managed a home with two small children after she lost her husband during the Vietnam War. Several years later she married a wonderful man by the name of Bill. He was the gift from God that she had prayed for.

To this day I am so grateful for having her as a part of my life in those days. She wiped away many tears in my disillusioned moments as a new wife and mother. She encouraged me when I doubted God and myself. She offered practical help when it was needed: like babysitting, picking me up for a women's event, or just having an attentive ear.

I remember her call one day inviting me to a women's meeting. She asked me to pray, before I came, about what woman I believed would be a good women's ministry leader for our new little church. I came to the meeting that night prepared to nominate Emilie. Upon my arrival to the meeting, being a few minutes late, I asked what had been discussed.

They all smiled and informed me that they had unanimously voted me as their first women's ministry leader.

I was honored by such a vote of confidence. However, at 23 years of age I had no experience and there were many ladies older than myself with years of expertise in this type of ministry. Before I could say "No, thank you" and decline this offer, Emilie stated, "God has called you to this ministry and we are going to help you."

From Emilie I learned:

• Recognize the character qualities of a true friend.

• Joy comes with a spirit of generosity.

• Adapt to your circumstances and you'll gain the ability to overcome obstacles.

Faye mentored me in my thirties. I stood in awe of this woman as she came to our church to be the first woman associate pastor. I was her personal assistant so I was able to observe her very closely. I saw that because of her grace and patience, God gave her great favor among the male associate pastors, who at first were set against her.

She reaffirmed the call on my life to women's ministries and encouraged me to be open to stepping back into ministry. Because of her loving encouragement, I took that step alongside her. She invested many hours developing my leadership gifts and sent me out with her full support to establish a new community women's Bible study in an area where we lived some years later. She is still serving the Lord today, now in her late eighties.

What I learned from Faye:

• Your faith will greatly increase as you step into places that at first seem difficult.

• Humility and grace will serve you well in the midst of trying circumstances.

Joy was my mentor in the late 1980s to the mid-1990s. I sought Joy's counsel after I recognized my sin of pride. I had thought so highly of myself that I just knew our new home church would love to hire me with all my past experience and qualifications, but all doors were slammed tightly shut.

I asked Joy how I could avoid falling into that pride again. As quickly as that question left my lips, she said, "Serve where you will not be noticed." The church we attended at that time further solidified her words. The series our pastor taught about the time Joy made that statement was on "servant leadership." It was a concept I had not yet learned in my first few years of leadership.

I found an opportunity to serve with the prison ministry team preparing food for women living in halfway houses. The team would visit the houses and minister while serving them a meal. For almost two years, that was the only ministry where I served, and I learned to love watching and seeing what God was doing in the lives of others. One day our leader approached me with an offer to go to Russia and minister in a women's prison. It was an opportunity to see God at work and be used by Him, speaking publicly once again. After a humbling yet insightful season of serving without being seen, I went to Russia with the right perspective of being used by God.

What I learned from Joy:

• Humble yourself and, in due time, God will lift you up.
• Persevere in righteousness. "Don't give up," she'd say. "God has a work for you to do."

Sharon has been a mentor in my life for the last decade. When I was employed by Women of Faith, she was my direct supervisor. We began traveling together because we both lived on the West Coast, and we spent hours together in airports, planes, and hotel rooms. When we were in our

hotel rooms, I often awoke in the morning to find her on her knees praying. She would repeat this habit again at night as we traveled across the
country. She boldly asked God for things I never thought to ask for—and
He answered!

For example, one cold winter day Sharon and several of us Women of
Faith representatives were sent to Kansas City, Kansas, to promote the
upcoming conference to the churches in that area. As we secured our rental
car and headed to our hotel, we tuned the radio to a local station. They
were broadcasting the weather. "We are expecting the worst snowstorm we
have seen in more than 25 years. It should last not more than three days.
Bundle up because the daily temperature will be severely cold."

We pulled into the parking lot of the hotel, and Sharon jumped out
of the car and extended her arms toward heaven and boldly prayed, "Lord,
we believe You have called us here to do Your work. We ask in the name
of Jesus that You will stay the snow until we have completed what You
have called us to do."

The next three days were bitter cold. However, we were successful in
reaching every church we had determined to visit during our time there.
On our way to return the rental car we stopped for gas. As I began pump-
ing, I brushed something white off my jacket. Then I heard someone
inside the car holler "It's snowing!" We returned the car and headed to the
airport. While waiting for takeoff I looked out my window and marveled
at God's answer to Sharon's prayer as the gentle snow was covering the tar-
mac just in time for our return home.

What I learned from Sharon:

- Believe in the power of prayer.
- Integrity will follow you all the days of your life.

As you can see, throughout the years God has used these mentors to
impart wise counsel and model Christlike living. From their own experi-

ences they expanded my view of life and God. They were better able to discern things about my situations than I was because they were emotionally detached, enabling them to have a clearer perspective. They believed in me, encouraged me, prayed for me, cried with me, and rejoiced with me whenever it was needed or appropriate. Because of their gifts and abilities, they have challenged me and caused me to grow in every aspect of my life.

Influence, just like salt

shaken out, is hard to see,

but its flavor is hard to miss.

—Pam Farrel

I have come to realize that while my mother orchestrated my life, revealing to me my gifts and talents, God has used my mentors to encourage and nurture those abilities.

Are You a Mentor?

As we mentioned earlier, you may be a mentor as well as a mom, though you may have never associated the word "mentor" with yourself. However, you may be a powerful influence in the lives of other women and/or your daughter's friends. Or perhaps you are a woman who has a heart for teenage girls and it's easy for you to communicate with them. You might team up with another mentor mom and she could take a group of Modern-Day Princesses, while you take another. She could have your daughter in her group, and her daughter could be in yours!

Some of the best mentors for a rite-of-passage journey have come from two main groups of women:

Group 1: These moms were introduced to a rite-of-passage journey and celebration because they wanted to give their own daughters the experience. They discovered that they loved the process so much that they committed to giving other young women the opportunity to be Modern-Day Princesses by leading other small groups.

Naomi is one of those women. Doreen and I would describe Naomi as enthusiastic and energizing. She took the Modern-Day Princess material and added to it. She tweaked some elements to dovetail and personalize it to the young women in her groups. She then added the option of the girls becoming DOKA (Daughters of the King Alumnae), which encourages young women to continue in this leadership discipleship and assist with future Modern-Day Princess groups.

I [Pam] first met Naomi over e-mail. Naomi wanted more information about the MDP ministry and permission to use the Teen Relationship Contract I developed. When I met her in person, one of the first things Naomi did was to pull out her pictures of the many groups of young women who had graduated from the Modern-Day Princess rite-of-passage ceremonies. The girls were dressed up, smiling, and wearing beautiful crowns.

What stood out the most to me was how the girls wanted to be in pictures with each other, in a BFF (best friends forever) kind of pose. In preparing for this book, Naomi had many of those girls on speed dial in her cell phone and the girls were eager to respond to any of Naomi's requests. It was obvious Naomi had been used by God to positively affect their lives and they were grateful to her for that.

Group 2: The other kind of leaders who tend to go on to have their own groups, and many more in succession, are those who have graduated from a Modern-Day Princess group or experienced some type of rite-of-passage ceremony. They know the value of mentoring and experiencing traditions, and are excited to give other girls this opportunity.

You might only facilitate a group once (maybe for your own daughter and her friends), but don't be surprised if you or your daughter enjoy it so much that one or both of you want to repeat the experience again and help other girls have this same wonderful experience. You may facilitate a group in the near future or if you've already gone through your own rite of passage, you might wait and facilitate a group for your little sister, a cousin, or someday, your own daughter or even your granddaughter!

As a mentor, you might feel you are walking a fine line between mother and daughter. Even if you are a mother who is running a Modern-Day Princess group, your role in the group will have you as the liaison, the mediator, the go-between person who needs to minister both to the "Queen Mother" and the promising princess. Because of my [Pam's] various life roles in ministry, I have been in this "middleman" position on numerous occasions. Sometimes I've found myself mentoring a mom and daughter at the same time in two different contexts. At other times, Mom was so pleased with the change discipleship made in her life, she wanted her daughter to experience it too.

The most challenging times are when I am discipling a daughter who is more mature spiritually or emotionally than her mother. In my role, I need to help the young woman honor her mother even when she might not be able to respect or fully obey her. In the following section we'll take a closer look at different mentoring situations you might encounter.

Styles of Mentoring

Daughter Solo: Let me [Pam] tackle the hardest mentoring context first. That is when the daughter, a princess, has a mom, a queen, who has abandoned her throne. God wants us to train young women to honor their fathers and mothers and learn to obey authorities. What does a daughter do when Mom's command is not a godly one?

For example, when I was in youth ministry full-time, there were a few scenarios where my mentee had made a purity vow to wait until marriage to have sex even though her own mother had one live-in boyfriend after another. Or, when I worked with Fellowship of Christian Athletes as an active mom mentor, there were girls who had taken the *One Way to Play* (no drugs, no drinking alcohol) even though their own mothers partied on wine and daiquiris, and were addicted to prescription drugs. In these times, part of your role is to exemplify what "healthy" looks like.

It is a challenge to help the daughter learn to obey the healthy things that her mother asks her to do and dismiss what is unhealthy and toxic that Mom might demand. You can help the daughter learn to say, "I love you, Mom. I value you, Mom, but on this one, I need to listen to God's voice instead of yours."

One young woman I worked with learned to refuse to buy her mother's cigarettes when her mom was too tired or drunk to get them herself. The daughter was being placed in an illegal and unhealthy position by her mother. Helping a girl learn, as best-selling author Rick Warren puts it, "to disagree without being disagreeable," is a noble goal. The resource *Boundaries*, by Drs. Cloud and Townsend, can be of great help to you as you train the young woman to respectfully respond to the ungodly, unhealthy environment that might be surrounding this "Cinderella."

Mother/daughter Duo: If you are in ministry or active in your local church, you might discover you are ministering to a mom in women's ministry and a daughter through a rite-of-passage program at the same time.

I found the secret of simultaneous mentoring is to treat each woman as an individual. To do this, it is critical to build high trust with the mother by ministering to her in a way that she would *know* that I have her best interests at heart. If I could accomplish that, she would usually conclude that I had her daughter's best interests at heart as well.

Over the years, I have learned to build trust with the daughter by keeping confidences, as long as life or liberties were not threatened. If there were a serious, life-altering issue at hand, we would both go together to her parents to deal with the situation. (An example would be if I knew a girl was suicidal, together we'd go to the parent(s) to get her further help.) In some situations, I offer the daughter choices:

"Do you want to talk to your mother about your sexual activity alone, or do you want me to come with you?"

"Do you want me to pray for you as you tell your folks in private that you (drank alcohol, did drugs, had an abortion, etc.), or do you want me to go with you?"

Teens tend to respect those adults who treat them as an adult rather than a child. Teens want the privileges of an adult, but they recognize they are being treated as an adult when you give them the responsibilities of one. I give the daughter the privilege of being an adult and handling a touchy, sensitive situation one-on-one with her parents. Yet, I offer myself as a safety net if she needs me to go with her to her parents or a counselor.

You are her mentor, not her counselor or her mother, so clearly share your boundaries in an empathetic and understanding way.

For most of the young women you will mentor, these extreme circumstances will *not* come up. For the most part, you are offering your mentorship to *prevent* a girl from ever making these choices or having to handle these kinds of life-altering situations. Some mentors, however, will be called to neighborhoods or community groups where the socioeconomic setting may mandate that you be prepared to deal with all kinds of inner-core character-building situations. If you prepare for the tough calls, the rest will feel like a piece of cake!

No matter what method of mentoring, you might find yourself in the place of a mom asking you to help her convince her daughter of something. I have found it is usually something I also think is important (like wise moral choices), but sometimes the issue is not something you will agree with or you might not have an opinion on.

If you differ from Mom's point of view, remember it is Mom and Dad who have ultimate accountability before God for their child's rearing so simply be honest and say something like, "Let me pray about that with you," "If you want, I'd be glad to be a sounding board to you if you want my input," or "If you'd like, I can give you some referrals of others (moms, parents, professionals) who might have insights for you."

For some issues, all you might do is pray, listen to both sides, and encourage parent and teen to discuss. It is amazing what you can accomplish if you point both parties to God's Word, prayer, and conversation. Often your role as mentor is simply to live out the call that was said of the prophet Elijah: "He will convince parents to look after their children and children to look up to their parents. . . ." (Malachi 4:6, MSG).

Remember, when in doubt, love always wins out (1 Corinthians 13:8). In James 1:5 (NASB), the Bible recommends, "If any of you lacks wisdom, let him ask of God, who gives to all generously. . . ." Whenever I don't know what to do, I ask:

- How would God show love in this situation?
- What characteristic of God can I best emulate that might bring hope, help, or healing in this situation?
- Is there someone more qualified or more experienced that I should recommend to this family?

As a mentor, you will influence with your words, so select them carefully; you will influence with your life, so walk it prudently; you will influence with your love, so give it lavishly.

Choosing a Mentor

Mothers most often coordinate their daughter's rite of passage. One of the first and most important steps you, as a mother, will take to prepare the way for your daughter's rite-of-passage journey is to find a woman (or women) you trust to become her mentor(s). Look for women who will say some of the things you will say to your daughter, or want to say but haven't had the opportunity to yet.

As we've mentioned before, select a mentor who might fill in gaps you cannot fill. For example, if you didn't finish college but are hoping your daughter does, you may look for a woman working on her degree or a woman with a graduate degree.

More than anything, you will be looking for a woman (or women) of character and compassion. Seek a woman who loves God and loves your daughter and wants to team with you to provide a strong future for your daughter and her friends.

When selecting mentors, you can do so informally over a cup of coffee. You can do what some moms did with Pam when she was working in youth ministry.

Karen's mom simply invited me [Pam] over for lunch and asked me to be involved in her daughter's life. Over a pot of spaghetti at a youth event at her home, Brenda's mom asked me to team with her. Teresa's mom talked to me in the apartment parking lot we both shared. It isn't the place so much that mattered, but the words of affirmation and encouragement they gave.

> *Successful people turn everyone who can help them into sometime mentors!*
>
> —JOHN C. CROSBY

Each shared her hopes and dreams for her daughter and asked me to spend a little extra time with her.

What I appreciate most, now that I am a parent, is that they "checked me out." They asked questions about my life, about my beliefs in key areas, about my plans that included their daughters, and about the manner and method by which I would influence them.

Other mentoring models can be more formalized, like the method Naomi, a mom in the MDP program, did with and for her daughter's mentors:

> Back in January I [Naomi] asked Amanda a series of questions to help her choose her mentors. I asked her to think about all the women she knew and then to consider:
> - Which ones do you admire the most?
> - Which women would you like to be like when you grow up?
> - Who would you like to be able to seek advice from for the next 10 years of your life?
> - What women do you know who have had a spiritual impact on your life and who model spiritual disciplines?

At Amanda's ceremony, her mom introduced the women Amanda had chosen to mentor her. See, through Naomi's introduction, how these women poured themselves into Amanda:

> This very special group of women was chosen by Amanda and have shared their wisdom with her in an area of discipline. I am so grateful that each one of these precious women has given to Amanda. So much of who Amanda is today, as well as who she

will be in the future, is directly related to the gifts and talents of these women.

- Dianna taught her how to sing.
- Krista spent several Tuesday mornings preparing her for her mission trip by teaching her a dance. She also spent a full day cooking with her.
- Beth's topic dealt with being a godly wife so she took Amanda out for a time of pampering and lunch. Beth has been a constant reminder of faithfulness to spouse, church, and family.
- Janee took her on a mission trip to Great Britain.
- Robin introduced her to acting.
- Terri taught her to love history.
- Penny taught her everything else.
- Andrea has been an example of what it means to be a godly friend.

Each one of these women gave to Amanda their most valuable commodity: their time and energy! It's true, love really is spelled T-I-M-E. We are so grateful to each of you.

—Graciously submitted by Mrs. Naomi S.

The Qualities of a Mentor

As you and your daughter consider a woman mentor, you may identify women whom you already recognize as mentors in your own life or your daughter's. For your daughter it may be a teacher, coach, youth leader, close friend, or family member (such as an older cousin or aunt). If you don't see a mentor in your daughter's life at this present time, we encourage you to begin praying that God will bring one into her life.

Releasing our daughters into the care of a mentor honors her highly. It means we (mothers) trust and respect this woman and are secure in the knowledge that she is like-minded and will uphold our standards of godliness and integrity.

Following are qualities that are important in a good mentor. She becomes:

- A friend—she will walk alongside your daughter and encourage, believe in, and laugh with her.
- A confident counselor—she is trustworthy with all that is spoken to her.
- A guide/coach—she assists in helping your daughter establish godly life skills in her relationship with God and others.

More specific things to consider in a mentor can be identified by this simple acrostic. A mentor is a woman who:

Makes God's Word a priority and uses Scripture to direct your daughter, not just her personal opinion.

Encourages the development of strengths, and challenges your daughter to overcome weaknesses.

Nurtures through prayer and seeks God's direction with and for your daughter.

Tactfully confronts in love when wrong thinking or actions are evident.

Obeys God and lives so that her spiritual walk with Him is evident to and confirmed by others.

Realizes that transparency and authenticity are strategic tools in mentoring. By sharing her strengths and potential weaknesses, she can help your daughter make wise decisions.

Mentor Moment

Earlier in this book, you heard from Debe, Karly's mom. Karly is one of the young women I [Pam] have had the pleasure of mentoring. Below are a few thoughts from Karly on her view of how vital it is to have a mentor:

I met Pam when I was 11 or 12 years old. The first thing that drew me to her was her fun, outgoing personality—and her babies. She had two young boys and one on the way. I started to go everywhere with Pam and helped her with her kids. I felt like a part of the family. It was really neat because I knew she cared, loved, and wanted to invest in me. It was obvious that I was a priority to her. She spent time talking to me about life, decisions, school, family, etc.

The thing that was even more important to me was the way she listened and encouraged me, especially in areas I was gifted in. She gave me godly direction and I took everything in like a sponge. I felt very comfortable with Pam and her words of advice. I looked up to her. She was a good mom, a good wife, and had so many goals and lived a BIG life. I wanted to be like her one day.

I don't think I ever feared that Pam would disclose information to my mother that I did not want her to know. I felt a trust in our relationship. It honestly did not even cross my mind. I never really considered Pam to be my mother's mentor; to me they were good friends. I had a very close relationship with my mom, so most of what I told Pam, my mom already knew. I was very blessed to have a mom who loved the Lord and was in many ways a mentor to me as well.

Another benefit of talking with Pam was that she had a way of making me feel safe and was able to be somewhat objective. With my mom . . . sometimes it was too emotional or we were too close to talk things out without feeling like I had to please her in my choices. (Of course I always wanted to.) Sometimes it was just easier to think on my own with Pam.

I feel very blessed to have had Pam as a mentor. I think I made some much braver and bolder choices because of having her in my life. She believed in me and made me feel like what I had to offer was important. She made BIG deals out of things that made me grow in my confidence. She attended events that were important to me: graduation, concerts I sang in, programs I directed, and so on. She was there for me. She prayed with and for me. She held me accountable.

One of the most life-changing memories with Pam was when she took me to a conference for young girls that taught about purity in relationships. I made a commitment that day to keep myself pure for my husband-to-be. I signed a contract and was given a key that I was to give to my husband the night of my wedding.

When your mentor lives what she teaches and is

authentic, it's much easier to stay on the right path and believe it's possible. Other women that I once considered mentors have since fallen off that path and have been disappointing. Pam and my mom are the only two women I know who have truly lived out the things they've encouraged me to be.

I didn't get married until I was 25 and I kept my covenant with God. The night of my wedding, I presented the key to my husband. To this day when I call Pam she calls back. Even though God takes her all over the world and she is beyond busy—she always carves time out for me. Now I'm in the place she was when we met. Now, I have three kids (and another baby on the way!). I don't know how she did it! I admire her even more, knowing that she had a crazy life but still made time to pour into me!

I'll probably still be looking to Pam for example and wisdom when my kids are teenagers and when I have grandkids too. I also have a passion now for mentoring young girls. I want to make the same kind of impact on their lives that Pam made on mine.

Remember, mentoring is something that often goes full circle, generation to generation. By investing in a young woman's life, you give her the tools and confidence to invest in others along her path.

7

Celebrate Your Modern-Day Princess!

Remember me, GOD, when you enjoy your people;
include me when you save them; I want to see
your chosen succeed, celebrate with your celebrating nation,
join the Hallelujahs of your pride and joy!

—PSALM 106:4–5 (MSG)

Oh, well, what's a royal ball? I suppose it would be frightfully
dull, and boring, and completely . . . completely *wonderful.*

—CINDERELLA (1950)

Imagine with me [Doreen] for a moment that we are attending a Modern-Day Princess ceremony. There is a center aisle decorated with royal-colored balloons on each side—purple, green, gold, and silver. In the center of the stage there is an overstuffed, regal-looking chair with a light flowing canopy draped high above. Flowers dress the edge of the stage. With all the regalia, it appears to be a king's throne. The audience will soon be asked to imagine that the King of Kings is sitting on that throne, delighted to preside over this celebration of His daughters and the knights who would bless them.

Instrumental worship music plays as the guests are ushered in. Right on time, the emcee introduces herself and thanks everyone who has participated to make this celebration come to fruition. Without further delay she announces, "Now, let this celebration begin!" The processional music reverberates and the back doors of the chapel swing open. The first young lady leads the march of the princesses down the center aisle. Many of the girls walk nervously yet most smile shyly as they meet the eyes of family and friends. The girls file in next to their fathers on the front row. Like a well-planned cadence, all the fathers and daughters sit down simultaneously.

The emcee personally introduces each girl, and her father or her "step-in" dad then escorts her to the podium. Each girl is given the microphone to share the class she enjoyed most and her favorite verse. In turn, the daughter hands the microphone to her father or "step-in" dad. Some of the men try to hide the fact that they are just as nervous as their daughters as they each bring their notes to rest on the podium. However, that first look into their precious girl's eyes often settles their nerves.

They each pronounce their blessing and crown each girl as a daughter of the King, a true Modern-Day Princess. They then return to their seats, often more warmly entangled arm in arm than when they arrived.

After all the girls are blessed and crowned, the emcee asks them to stand and look toward her. She then addresses the crowd of proud and excited parents and friends: "If you are willing to support these young ladies in their journey into womanhood, please stand." The girls are asked to turn and look to see who is standing. With excited hearts, the daughters see the teary but smiling and twinkling eyes of their supportive network of family and friends.

The fathers and daughters line up in front of the stage, forming a receiving line. The ushers stand at each pew, allowing the opportunity for everyone to come up and shake hands or extend hugs to these special dads and daughters. This is a celebration for a Modern-Day Princess!

You've read examples of family and private rite-of-passage celebrations, but this chapter is an outline of what might happen at a group rite-of-passage ceremony. After each girl has worked hard journeying through her rite of passage, she experiences the crowning conclusion—or rather, the new beginning of her life as she steps across the threshold of womanhood. This is an excellent reason to party!

Walking Out the Front Gates

Wouldn't it be wonderful if every girl between the ages of 12 and 21 had a preparation-for-womanhood course and a celebration of her passage into womanhood? Imagine with us the number of confident, poised, prayerful young women of influence who could be regularly released into society to make a positive imprint on the world. Instead of counseling offices filled with women dealing with father issues, Congress could be filled with daughters carrying out the goals of their Heavenly Father. Instead of marriages broken over unresolved problems, records could be broken in a multitude of areas such as science, sports, academics, and maybe even world peace.

The rite-of-passage ceremony is much more than a nice little party; it is the calling and commissioning of females to walk out their Heavenly Father's plans, passions, and path. The rite-of-passage ceremony is indeed the "crowning" moment. Presidents have inaugurations, pastors have ordination services, military officers have commissionings; shouldn't a young man or young woman have a ceremony that celebrates his or her step into the responsibilities and privileges of the adult world?

Oh, What a Knight!

In the book *Raising a Modern-Day Knight*, author Robert Lewis writes of the path of a Modern-Day Knight:

> Sons need fathers who are involved in their lives—dads who will love them, teach them, and discipline them. But clearly, sons also need a masculine vision. They need a manhood language. They need a ceremony. And they need other men. Knighthood, as an outline, offers all this and more.
>
> First, the Knight embodied a well-defined set of ideals. Many knights sincerely adhered to and embraced a moral code of honor. They pledged themselves to their lord, their king and their God. . . . Many knights also became *milites Christi*, "Knights of Christ." As such, they believed they bore responsibilities to the kingdom of God and to society as a whole . . . This chivalric code of honor formed the moral and social bedrock of noble life. . . .
>
> I will assist you, as a father, in formulating three specific ideals for your son: a vision for manhood, a code of conduct, and a transcendent cause. . . . There is a second reason why the medieval knight speaks to the modern boy's journey to manhood . . . his life also outlined a well-defined process. The boy who pursued knighthood followed a clearly marked path.[1]

Let's Hear It For the Girls!

If we believe boys should be well prepared for manhood, it is obviously reasonable that young women should be prepared to join them in the adult world. We know that almost every little girl dreams of being a princess at some point in her life. How grand if upon her transition into womanhood, she received her crown and recognized and accepted all the responsibilities and privileges that accompany being a godly woman, a daughter of the King.

Moving into the Moment!

The day of the actual celebration is the coronation of her rite of passage. Your daughter will be giddy with excitement because so much work and preparation has been invested in preparing for this moment.

To better understand the meaning of the event, let's look closer at the elements of the ceremony. This is an outline of what might happen at a Modern-Day Princess ceremony and celebration, but many of the elements can also be adapted for a public or private party sponsored by a single family as well.

The Preparation

I [Doreen] can confidently say, along with other mentors and facilitators of MDP groups, that one of the most rewarding moments is watching what has been taught put into action. Preparation time just prior to the ceremony enables us to see, quite often, how our emphasis on using makeup to enhance their beauty is ultimately applied. Our consensus as facilitators has been that every girl glows first from a radiance from within, and second from their natural beauty that has been gently enhanced.

Their etiquette training is often revealed when a formal dinner is served and the girls begin sharing with their families what fork to use, how many inches they should be sitting from the table, and so on.

I believe this is one of the most exciting parts of the journey for mothers and mentors as well as the girls. Preparation for a more formal ceremony brings reality to what every girl has dreamed of, and it's also a fulfillment of a parent's dream for his or her daughter as well. This might look different for different groups, but the result is the same. One group of girls agreed together that they would all wear simple spring dresses and have the ceremony in the lovely backyard where their weekend retreat was held.

The fun came when the girls gathered in the host family's bathrooms to do their makeup. They had received tips from a makeup artist just the day before so they were excitedly using some of the cosmetics their moms had allowed them to purchase and heeded her suggestions. The high level of laughter, oohs, and ahhs filled the house just minutes before the "Butterfly Kisses" song filled the living room. They entered in all their natural beauty, filing in to stand and then sit next to their fathers.

For other girls and groups, it was the first time they would wear makeup, get their nails professionally manicured, have an up-do hairstyle done by a professional, or shop for a "formal" dress.

The Grand Entrance

As in a wedding procession, each of the beautiful young girls enters an auditorium, possibly a living room, or maybe a beautiful backyard. They walk single file down an aisle or into a room while music (an inspirational song she or the group has chosen) plays triumphantly. (Use a song that has special meaning to the girls.) One by one, they gracefully pass family and friends standing with wowed and smiling faces that display their encouragement and enthusiastic approval to these young ladies who will be honored this day.

One parent shares his emotional response to seeing his daughter at this point in the ceremony:

> When I saw her come down the aisle, I knew I was doomed. She had me—lock, stock, and barrel. She was so beautiful and yet so

young. The dress, makeup, and glitter said I'm 22 years old, but in her eyes I could see the innocence of my 12-year-old and how much she needed me. My love for her overwhelmed me. In my heart, I swore I would more than "just be there" for her. I would be her knight in shining armor; the one to take her on dates; the one she would compare all the potential boyfriends to. I would do anything to protect her, be the father she needed me to be, preserve her purity.

These commitments to my daughter hit me all at once as she came down the aisle. Our turn came to stand at the podium and I publicly pronounced my blessing to her. I could barely get the words out through all my tears. It was all so incredible.

The truly amazing thing came weeks, months, and now years following that moment. She changed. Our relationship changed. I could not explain why but she was different. Prior to the ceremony, when I would correct her she would run down the hall devastated, saying things like, "You don't love me!" "How could you hurt me like this?" "Why do you hate me?" As her father (and a guy) I didn't get this. I could not seem to reassure her enough of my love for her.

I would think, *I am willing to die for you. How can you even think that?* I spent much of the time feeling very misunderstood.

After the ceremony, the first time I corrected her she responded with, "Okay, Daddy," then turned and quietly walked away. I had prepared myself for an emotional explosion. I sat there and stared at where she had stood, thinking, *What just happened?* I was speechless.

A few weeks later, she and I were talking and I asked her about this change. She said, "Well, Daddy, I didn't believe you loved me. Every time you corrected me, it felt like you hated me and you were punishing me because you didn't like me."

I responded, "But I've told you a thousand times that I love you; it is your behavior I don't like."

She stated, "I know, but I didn't believe you."

"So what is different? Why do you believe me now?" I asked.

"When you stood up in front of all those people and said you loved me and why you loved me, well, that's when I knew it was real. Now I know you really do love me."

That was two years ago.

Recently (Jess is now 14 years old) she was leaving to go spend the night at a friend's house. She came to hug me good-bye, then pressed in and said, "I'm going to miss you, Daddy."

I countered, "I will miss you too, sweetheart. Have the best time."

She happily replied, "I will. You can call me to say good night if you want." I held back my tears as the authenticity of her heartfelt understanding of my love for her was evident.

If we had not participated in this ceremony, we would not have gained all that it has meant to us. Its effects didn't just last a week, a month, or even a year. I am still reaping the benefits of this public declaration. She still believes I love her.

—Robert B.

The Introduction

The Master of Ceremonies, or parent facilitator, enthusiastically introduces each princess, announcing the young lady's name and its meaning, her age, and something personal she has observed or been told about the young lady.

There is purpose to each piece of the ceremony. Validating these young ladies publicly is of key importance to them at this stage of their lives. They are constantly reminded by peers and the media what the "perfect girl" is to look and act like. As parents, leaders, and mentors, our affirmation to them is extremely valuable, whether they appear to appreciate it or not.

Lorri, an eighth-grade teacher, facilitated the program in her Christian school. She and her co-facilitator each made several introductions for their group of girls. It was evident they had taken the time to create a personal introduction for each girl. Here is one of Lorri's introductions:

> *Parents can only give good advice or put their children on the right paths, but the final forming of a person's character lies in their own hands.*
>
> —ANNE FRANK

Bethany Joy Vigil was born on August 10, 1991, to Timothy and Rita Vigil.

Bethany's name means House of God.

Having been Bethany's teacher, I can honestly say that Bethany has allowed her heart to be the House of God and lives up to her name. Some of the qualities that I have observed in Bethany are excellence, faithfulness, and humility. One of the virtues a princess must possess is humility.

Bethany does not demand or expect special treatment even though she has been a straight-A student since third grade. She chooses to refrain from bragging about her accomplishments, but is eager to help those who are struggling. Bethany does not have to be in the spotlight because she already knows she is a princess.

The verse I chose for Bethany is Psalm 149:4, "For the LORD takes delight in his people; he crowns the humble with salvation."

The Princess's Address

The emcee then invites each girl to share something she learned along her journey in preparation for this celebration. If it is a biblically based program, the young lady is encouraged to share her favorite Scripture verse and explain why she selected it. Here are a few of some Modern-Day Princesses' selections as examples:

My favorite Bible verse was Psalm 139:8: "If I go up to the heavens, you are there; if I make my bed in the depths, you are there." It was our very first memory verse in the class.

That verse is really important to me because it is a reminder that I can't go away from God's presence or His love. Any time I feel I have no one, He is always right there.

My favorite class was Faith vs. Feeling. We were to journal our feelings every morning. Then every night we would write how we had gone about our day, whether we acted out by our feelings or our faith. God revealed a lot to me during that week. He showed me that in everything that I had done, I acted on my feelings, not with Him. I need to rely on Him and His Word, not my feelings because they are kind of crazy.

—Carina

My favorite verse is Psalm 91:1–2, "He who dwells in the shelter of the Most High will rest in the shadow of the Almighty. I will say of the LORD, 'He is my refuge and my fortress, my God, in whom I trust.'"

When I was growing up, my parents always told me, "When you are afraid, say this verse." I was afraid a lot, so that's why I love that verse.

Going through this class gave me another meaning for this verse. God is my authority and He ordains people in my life to be my authority, and as soon as I step outside that authority, He is no longer my refuge or my fortress. I am no longer abiding in His shadow. This class challenged me to make sure, even though I'm 18 now and I can vote, I still need to obey my parents and other authorities He places in my life, but most importantly Him.

I liked the Makeup & Manners class because I'd always get stains on my new shirts when I ate soup. I learned in the class that you scoop away from you instead of toward your bowl. Now I can go out to restaurants and wear new shirts and I won't get stains on them!

—Erica

The Blessing

A rite-of-passage ceremony, whether done as a family or as a group, should always include the proclaiming of the promise of a bright future over the princess. If it can be done by many people at the celebration—Dad, Mom, mentor, friends, and family—all the better!

One powerful way to ensure the promise or potential is verbally shared with a princess is to include in the ceremony a specific time for this. It might be affirmations read by mentors and moms, or cards of encouragement given by friends and family, but it should always include a verbal blessing by her father or her "step-in" dad.

In the MDP group celebration, each father, or another significant man, steps forward to impart his blessing personally over his daughter. He praises her character and abilities, shares his vision for her future, and prays for God's blessing over her life. The emotion attached to what he shares often brings him and her to tears (and those in the audience!). Arielle, a Modern-Day Princess, shares her thoughts below:

When our Night of Celebration came I was so excited and nervous! I was number 7 in the line of 10 girls. The dads said their blessings and then the girls shared about their experiences and their favorite verse. My blessing was three pages long! I would like to share just a few different things from my blessing.

In my list of favorite things of nature I put the beach. Here is what my dad said in my blessing: "At the beach the shoreline changes. Daily storms come and bring debris and destruction but they do not last. People are drawn to experience the beach. The beauty is never impacted for very long because the draw to the beach is not so much the sand and water, but rather the combination of the ocean and its shore.

"Your ocean is God Himself and He moves on you daily, bringing change and growth in you. You are His shoreline. Every person that 'visits' you will be captured by the expression of the Lord Almighty and what He has done in your life."

One of the other favorite things in my blessing was about gentleness, as in the manner in which a lioness deals with her cubs. "She is gentle when she encounters those things life brings to her. You are gentle as you encounter all that life brings to you." The reason I like this is because my name means Lioness of God and I thought what he said about that was so awesome!

Thank you so much for letting me share my personal story about how Daughters of the King has impacted me for life. I will never be the same since taking this class!

—Arielle

Receiving Her Crown

Finally, the pinnacle moment arrives. Dad faces his daughter, places the tiara on her head, and proclaims her a "Modern-Day Princess" (some faith-based groups choose to announce the girl as a "Daughter of the King") to the cheers of those in the audience. Beaming with pride, the "blessed" young woman returns arm in arm with her father to her seat, and the ceremony continues for the next young lady.

This blessing can profoundly change the attitude and course of a young girl's life.

❧

Sienna was angry when she entered the first class. She was late because she didn't want to be there. She said her parents had forced her to take the class. However, after realizing that a few friends were also participating, she became comfortable and engaging within a couple of weeks.

Her anger toward her father was still clearly evident as we began to discuss who would impart her blessing. She said she really didn't want her dad to do it but felt she didn't have much of a choice. Still, her excitement about the celebration managed to detour her anger and fears.

The Night of Celebration soon arrived. Sienna looked beautiful as she walked down the aisle with a sweet but tense smile. She filed in next to her dad and sat with her arms at her side. When she and her father were called to the podium, he extended his arm to escort her to the front. She stated her participation in the class quickly and handed him the microphone. He began reminiscing several fond memories of her and humorously recalled a moment they had together when they had mountain climbed together. That cool and cautious look broke as Sienna giggled.

His further warm words of affirmation melted her heart. As he crowned her, he leaned down and hugged her. She immediately embraced him in return. As they turned toward the audience, Sienna smiled with delight. When they sat down together, she wrapped her arm in his for the rest of the celebration. It was clear that she had regained some trust and respect for her dad that night, along with the realization that he really did love her.

Her mom told me [Doreen] days later that Sienna came and thanked her for all she did to make this an amazing celebration for her and her friends. Her mom could hardly believe what she had heard.

I have found that at every celebration I have facilitated or attended, women of all ages (2 to 92!) desire to be crowned a princess. They make comments such as "I wish I could have experienced this as a teenager." Or, "I still want to be a princess." Or, "I still would love to be crowned and affirmed by my father, and I'm 35!"

A rite-of-passage ceremony delivers the opportunity for a teenage girl to receive her own "real" crown and celebrate her beauty within. This is *her* moment, when she is seen by everyone as a lovely young woman. The ceremony provides her with the joy of being publicly crowned by a man she has chosen to impart her blessing. Most importantly, she acknowledges and believes God's wonderful identity of her: someone worthy to be cherished, loved, and valued, and someone who loves, cherishes, and values others and the principles close to her Abba Father's heart.

See, it is not the program or schedule that is powerful—it is the words of blessing and affirmation that bring an atmosphere of celebration. The jubilation comes from watching a young woman embrace her identity in Christ. If you know God's Word, you know the power that comes when one sees herself as God sees her. It is truly beautiful to watch firsthand as a young lady steps into her promising future and, with the support and encouragement of those who love her, embraces womanhood with purpose and confidence.

The Reception Party

Moms and daughters, as you have already read, have fun through the entire rite-of-passage journey—the preparation, mentoring, and so on—to the day of the ceremony and celebration. Dads and daughters have incredible healing and heartfelt moments during the blessing and throughout the celebration.

One particular addition that has been made to some of the celebrations is the father/daughter dance (for groups comfortable with this). After the cake-cutting, the fathers are called to stand in the middle of the dance floor. A special father/daughter song begins to play as they extend their hands to their daughters to come and dance this first dance.

In addition, the fathers are contacted a couple of weeks prior to the celebration and asked if they have a song they'd like to dedicate to their daughters. The girls are quite surprised when it is announced by the emcee that their father, or "step-in" dad, has dedicated a special song to her. The evening is seasoned with these songs as well as other favorites that the girls have requested. (The song choices can be approved by those hosting the event.) Attendees have commented that this addition to the party has added many more wonderful memories for everyone who has participated.

Following is the frequent and wonderful experience of the party and the results thereafter. Here is my [Doreen's] reflection of one ceremony celebration:

Some of the moms have done a fabulous job of decorating the room where the party will be taking place. Other moms help put together the delicious treats that are tastefully displayed and ready to eat. The girls' bouquets grace the table where the cake is placed, ready for pictures. The princesses arrive with many cheers as they are led to the cake table. They all lean in touching the cutting knife for one of those "all together" pictures. It feels like a paparazzi moment with all the cameras flashing. Usually, a guest proposes a toast and you hear the clinking of punch glasses, cheers, and laughter.

As a leader, I mingle among the crowd and overhear comments such as, "She is just beautiful, you must be so proud," "She is so grown up; where did the years go?" "I wish I could have had this when I was a girl," "This is amazing! I've never seen or heard of anything like this," and "I've never seen so many men cry! Every one of those blessings touched me." Or people ask me, "Have you ever considered doing this for women? I'd still like to be blessed by my father or a man of integrity in my life."

Treasure the Memory in Your Heart

Just as Mary, the mother of Jesus, "treasured up all these things and pondered them in her heart" (Luke 2:19), all parents who create and participate in a rite-of-passage ceremony help form memories that last a lifetime for themselves and their daughters. This is one mother's treasure box full of memories of her daughter's rite-of-passage experience:

Dear Doreen,

I'd like to share with you about my daughter, Catherine.

Catherine had always dreamed of being a princess as a little girl. We bought her a petite tiara and jewelry gift set to wear with the beautiful princess dress that she received from her grandmother and her Aunt Clare. I remember that she loved to twirl around while she stood in front of a mirror for hours.

As the years passed, when she'd worn out her play crowns we would get her more until they no longer fit her head.

She wanted us to buy a new house with two big sets of stairs coming down into a grand ballroom like the castles she saw in Cinderella, Snow White, Beauty and the Beast, *and many other movies that portrayed the princess theme. As she became a teenager, her body was growing up but in her heart she still desired to be a princess. She watched* The Princess Diaries *and once again said her dream home is a mansion!*

In spring, 2004, she entered the Ms. Northern New Mexico Teenage Pageant held in Pecos, New Mexico. She stood tall, so beautiful in her long formal gown. She was announced as the second runner-up but there was a mistake so she did not win the title. I thought she would be heartbroken. I know I was. When the girls left the stage, I was there to greet her because I thought she would be in tears. However, I found her consoling the other three girls who did not win and congratulating the winners! I was so proud to be her mom.

She always asked me, "Am I a princess?" I would tell her, "No, your daddy is not a king." Well, did I have a lesson to learn! During Catherine's celebration, I wept as I saw my daughter have her dream come true when her father placed the tiara on her head. I want you to know that, since her celebration, there is within Catherine a sense of complete confidence that she is now truly a princess. In her own words she said to me recently, "I know I am now a Princess of God."

Funny, as I write this, I remembered that when I was dating and first married my husband, Bill (now of 25 years), I called him Prince William, and today he is the king of our castle. Thanks, Doreen, for letting us see today that our family is one of true royalty!

Sincerely,

The McSweeney Family

It's the Thought, Not the Price Tag, That Counts

You might be seeing a sizable expense in the rite-of-passage celebrations that have been mentioned. However, as we've stressed, this journey can be done at no cost or a very low cost. The main principle should not be lost in all the decorations, dresses, and detailed touches. Remember that the core message is about a journey to womanhood that pinnacles with a celebration, not the cost of that celebration. If you desire to celebrate your daughter's journey but are concerned about the expense, here are a few more of my [Doreen's] suggestions:

- In your first session—use handmade cards for distribution of her affirmation cards to local family and friends. Therefore no postage is necessary.

- Use handmade cards, using fun stamps and stickers, for her distribution of cards to her father or step-in dad, and to her friends.
- A makeup session can be done with Mom's available cosmetics, or a friend who may be a beauty consultant might give you and your daughter a makeover for free.
- Invitations to her celebration can also be handmade or printed on the family computer printer. This can be quite fun and beautiful!
- Her celebration can be right in your own home by asking a limited number of family and friends to attend and making it a potluck. (This is one other way to pass on a legacy of womanhood—have each woman in the family and friendship circle make her favorite dish and bring the recipe to give the princess!)
- Your daughter could wear her favorite dress (it doesn't have to be a formal) and you could provide her with a simple piece of special jewelry from your collection, Mom.
- You could possibly borrow a tiara from someone who has been a prom queen or has gone through the Modern-Day Princess program. (This might be the one place you spend a little money.)
- Cut some flowers from your garden for her bouquet.
- Dad could wear a tie he already owns—or he can borrow one!
- You can bake a homemade cake with her name on it and have it say "You've Become a Modern-Day Princess!"
- Make sure someone has a camera and is taking pictures. Mom, you can even use some of your old, unused costume jewelry to decorate a frame for a favorite photo as a memento of the celebration.

There you have it—a low-cost rite of passage that is filled with meaning and memories!

The Love Lingers

After every party, no matter how the rite of passage is celebrated, elaborately or simply, the crowd wants to linger in the love they have all witnessed and experienced. Eventually, the crowd will begin to dwindle and the girls will hug and give air kisses to one another on the cheek. As they say good-bye, I [Doreen] usually hear, "I'll call you!" or "Text me!" As the evening comes to a close, many of these precious girls will place their crowns strategically in their rooms to be the last thing they see as they close their eyes to sleep and the first thing they see as they awake in the morning, reminding them that they are true Modern-Day Princesses.

Mentoring Moment

Prayer is a powerful way to bless a young woman. In our book *Got Teens?*, Jill Savage, the founder of Hearts at Home, and I [Pam] explain more on the power of parenting by faith. I like to take that principle one step further by regularly praying by faith. Praying by faith means I select and pray verses for my child or my mentee—not reflective of who she is *now* but *who I believe God wants her to be*, who God is calling her to be.

Hebrews 11:1 (NASB) says, "Now faith is the assurance of things hoped for, the conviction of things not seen." In Philippians 1:6 (NASB) we are encouraged to be people of faith like Paul, who said, "For I am confident of this very thing, that He who began a good work in you will perfect it until the day of

Christ Jesus." She will grow into her crown. As you pray, you and your daughter or mentee will see the changes that God will bring.

For a few of you reading this, you might be dealing with a young woman who has made a series of poor choices. I encourage you to look to Abraham as an example of the kind of faith you will need to develop. Romans 4:17 (NASB) gives this beautiful description of God: ". . . God, who gives life to the dead and calls into being that which does not exist." The context of this scripture is the story of Abraham. And the next few verses explain even better what faith looks like:

> In hope against hope [Abraham] believed, so that he might become a father of many nations according to that which had been spoken, "So shall your descendants be."
>
> Without becoming weak in faith he contemplated his own body, now as good as dead since he was about a hundred years old, and the deadness of Sarah's womb; yet, with respect to the promise of God, he did not waver in unbelief but grew strong in faith, giving glory to God, and being fully assured that what God had promised, He was able also to perform. Therefore it was also credited to him as righteousness. (Romans 4:18–22, NASB)

This does not mean that we pray a few prayers like spiritual tokens in a heavenly slot machine and God pours out a jackpot. Rather, when we pray in faith, God helps us see our child, or mentee, from His perspective; and we begin to see the promise and potential in a person, rather than only seeing the problem.

In my book *Woman of Confidence*, I explain:

> While speaking out the truth is powerful, it is important to realize why it is powerful and what the focus needs to be. The strength of speaking the dream is NOT in your personality, pleading, or power. Just because you speak your adventure, doesn't mean it will happen. It is when you speak God's adventure over your life that all of who God is will be working in your direction. Picture God's dream as the subway system. When you catch God's train, you are going in God's direction for your life. When you catch God's train, you will be on the adventure of a lifetime.[2]

We want our young women to be on God's plan and path for their lives. This is the power of the Word, which God says is like a "light" unto her path (Psalm 119:105) and "a sword," judging the "thoughts and intentions of the heart," (Hebrews 4:12, NASB). Second Timothy 3:16–17 (NASB) tells us, "All Scripture is inspired by God and profitable for teaching, for reproof, for correction, for training in righteousness; so that the man of God may be adequate, equipped for every good work." Isn't that what you desire for your daughter or mentee—a life equipped for every good work?

In *The 10 Best Decisions a Woman Can Make*, I take a woman through an exercise for her own life, which captures the power of the Word. It is easily adapted to help you gather a set of verses you can pray over your daughter or mentee or use to create a letter of affirmation you can give to her on or after her rite-of-passage celebration. Here are the simple steps:

- List the fears or flaws of your princess.
- Ask, "What trait of God is opposite of that fear or flaw?" (For example, if I wrote *anxiety*, the opposite of that is peace.)
- Use a concordance or Web site (such as www.biblegate way.com) to look up verses with the key word in it.
- Select one or two favorite verses.
- Repeat the process for other fears or flaws (find the opposite trait of God for each word you listed in step 1).
- String the verses together and insert your daughter/mentee's name to personalize Scripture to her life.

Here's a simple example:

Step 1:

My daughter/mentee is

    Unforgiving

    A follower

    Shy

Steps 2–5:

She is unforgiving—God is gracious and full of mercy.

She is a follower—God is victorious, the head, leader, King.

She is shy—God is confident, valiant.

Step 6:

Favorite verses I selected for my daughter/mentee, strung together, and personalized. For example:

Pam is "kind and compassionate . . . forgiving . . . just as in Christ God forgave [her] (Ephesians 4:32). . . . in all these things [Pam is] more than [a conqueror] through him who loved [her]. (Romans 8:37) Such confidence as this is ours through Christ before God. Not that [Pam is] competent in [herself] to claim anything for [herself], but [her] competence comes from God. (2 Corinthians 3:4–5, based on NIV)

Can you imagine the power of an entire page of Scripture prayed and posted over a young woman's heart? Create a prayer of encouragement and affirmation and frame it for your daughter/mentee. Consider it a "royal decree" of the truth whispered over her life day after day as she lives out God's future for her life.

To the Man Who Will Impart Her Blessing: Words to Write for Your Princess

A wise man has great power, and a man
of knowledge increases strength.

—Proverbs 24:5

If I sat here for three or four weeks, I could
not adequately describe just how important
the father/daughter relationship is.

—Dr. James Dobson[1]

Why should a man impart a blessing? I [Doreen] remember when that question was first raised. It was from me. I had always envisioned a father imparting that blessing. However, my first class consisted of four girls, two of whom did not have the option of receiving a blessing from their father. When I began to research God's Word on the importance of a man imparting this blessing, I quickly discovered that blessings play a significant role in God's plan. All blessings recorded in the Old Testament were imparted by men:

- God, the Heavenly Father, imparted the first blessing upon Adam and Eve in Genesis 1:28: "God blessed them and said to them . . ."
- Isaac, the father of Jacob and Esau, imparted his blessing upon Jacob in Genesis 27:28–29: "May God give you . . . grain and new wine. May nations serve you. . . . May those who curse you be cursed and those who bless you be blessed."
- God's chosen leaders pronounced blessings. The priests, the sons of Levi, were chosen by God "to minister and to pronounce blessings in the name of the LORD" (Deuteronomy 21:5).

Throughout the Old Testament, it was God's ordained plan for a succession of priests to bless the people of God at significant moments in their life as a nation.

After the resurrection of Jesus, things changed significantly but the idea of a blessing continued. The blessing was given to every believer in the form of the Holy Spirit (Ephesians 1:3–14) who gave each of us free access to the throne of grace and eliminated the need for priests to represent the people before God. In a very real sense, every believer is a priest because we each have direct access to God's presence (Hebrews 4:16; 1 Peter 2:9). We, therefore, do not need another individual to represent us before God.

This change transported us all into the realm of influence. Since the Holy Spirit lives in every believer, our words, our actions, and our prayers help others grow in their faith and discover their giftedness. Hebrews 3:13 gives insight into the power of our influence on one another, "But encourage one another day after day, as long as it is still called 'Today,' so that none of you will be hardened by the deceitfulness of sin" (NASB).

Your encouragement in the lives of these young women will help keep their hearts soft and will help keep them out of deception. This applies to both moms and dads because, as believers, we all have the same Spirit living in us (Galatians 3:14).

This does not, however, mean that Dad's influence is the same as Mom's influence. In 1 Thessalonians 2:7–12, the apostle Paul gives his insight into the unique influence that moms and dads have on those around them. In verses 7–8, we discover the following characteristics of a mom's influence:

- She has a gentle influence on those she loves.
- She tenderly cares for her children.
- She has a fond affection for those she loves.
- She imparts truth to her family.
- She gives her life in sacrificial commitment.

In verses 9–12 (NASB), we see a different set of characteristics for a dad's influence:

- He works hard to take care of his family.
- He leads by example. His influence is strongest when it is "devout, upright and blameless."
- He exhorts, encourages, and implores his children (all three of these are primarily spoken words that motivate growth).
- His goal is that his children will "walk in a manner worthy of the God who calls you . . ."

As a result, a very powerful thing happens in the heart of a daughter when her dad (or a father figure) publicly proclaims a blessing over her. The impact of his "exhorting, and encouraging, and imploring" becomes active and mixes with the influence of the Holy Spirit to literally move the heart of the young lady who is receiving the blessing.

To be sure, there is a profound effect that takes place when Mom tenderly and sacrificially oversees all the preparation steps for the rite of passage and Dad provides a public proclamation. Intense spiritual growth takes place. That is why we see the fruit of these ceremonies flourish years after the event.

Guys, Take the Lead!

Men hold within themselves one of the most sought-after gifts in heaven and on earth: leadership! We look to those in leadership positions with awe and respect when they use their positions righteously. We quake in fear when they lord it over us unrighteously. This truth applies as much to a father in his own home as it does to the leader of a powerful nation. How men use this place of honor affects the lives of those they have been called to care for, be it millions or within the intimate structure of a family.

> *Expressing my love to my daughter brought me to tears; I now see her as a young woman and need to treat her that way.*
>
> —ROGER B., FATHER OF A MODERN-DAY PRINCESS

Today, women also hold positions of great leadership: prime ministers of nations, presidential candidates, governors, and heads of mighty corporations, yet even in the most powerful woman, there is a place in her heart only her father can fill. When a man becomes a father for the first time and holds his precious new baby in his arms, it can be one of the most incredible moments of his life as he looks at what he had the power to create—a new life. That same moment for the new father can often contain the sweeping fear and realization that this new life now carries great responsibility for years to come.

Pam's husband, Bill, shared that when he held their firstborn moments after his birth he thought, *He fits perfectly in my arm! This little baby is depending on ME for everything! Step up, Bill!* Chad, Doreen's husband, expressed similar feelings. When he held their firstborn daughter he had a sense of awe that he was part of the creation of this little person. Yet, he felt overwhelmed knowing that he would be responsible for all her needs for a very long time. The reality is that leadership always carries responsibility.

If your daughter is a teenager, you have potentially carried responsibility for her for anywhere from 12 to 18 years. You have provided a roof over her head, food on the table, and I'd bet you've even provided some of her "wants" along with her needs. Therefore, your current influence most often has been demonstrated in your daughter's life as provider, disciplinarian, and protector. However, the person who has probably had the greatest effect on your daughter thus far is Mom, because she has been her role model in what it means to be "a woman."

But things are about to change! Your "little girl" is coming of age and growing out of adolescence into young adulthood. Boys and, eventually, other men are going to be playing a bigger role in her life. It is important for you to remember that you have the most important "role" in her "play" at this stage in her life. She will be measuring every man—be it a teacher, coach, other dads, or boys (especially a boy who may turn into a boyfriend, fiancé, then husband!)—by the standard you have set before her. This is the biggest responsibility that comes with your role as a father: living out your life as a man of integrity.

Psalm 15 is a wonderful guideline within a biblically based program that describes a man of integrity. While preparing for her rite of passage, your daughter will be encouraged to read this psalm. She will be reminded that no man is perfect and that a man, young or old, who desires to be Christlike seeks to meet the standards of Psalm 15. Challenge your daughter to use that psalm as she evaluates her future male relationships.

For your convenience I've provided it for you here:

LORD, who may dwell in your sanctuary? Who may live on your holy hill? He whose walk is blameless and who does what is righteous, who speaks the truth from his heart and has no slander on his tongue, who does his neighbor no wrong and casts no slur on his fellowman, who despises a vile man but honors those who fear the LORD, who keeps his oath even when it hurts, who lends his money without usury and does not accept a bribe against the innocent. He who does these things will never be shaken. (Psalm 15)

Perhaps you, Dad, are thinking right about now: *I have not lived up to that!* or *How am I ever going to be able to follow that standard?* Don't despair! God promises that He will never give you a command, a responsibility, or a call on your life without giving you the power to carry it out. If you have not yet lived your life in this manner, it's not too late to start. If you feel like you've tried and failed over and over again, it's not too late to pick up the pieces and continue.

In Scripture, whenever God called forth man for a responsibility, He also equipped him with the power to fulfill it.

First Samuel 10:10 says that when Saul was called to be Israel's first king, "The Spirit of God came upon [Saul] in power . . ."

When Samuel anointed David to be God's chosen king: "The Spirit of the LORD came upon David in power . . ." (1 Samuel 16:13).

Luke 9:1–2 states when "Jesus had called the Twelve [disciples] together, he gave them power and authority to drive out all demons and to cure diseases, and he sent them out to preach the kingdom of God. . . ."

Second Timothy 1:7 says, "For God did not give us a spirit of timidity, but a spirit of power, of love and of self-discipline."

Dad, God has equipped you to be one of the biggest forces in your daughter's life and what an amazing calling that is!

The Old Testament presents a very clear pattern that it is God's desire that His children are blessed. God made sure of this when He appointed the tribe of Levites to become the priests of Israel, according to Deuteronomy 10:8, "to stand before the Lord to minister and to pronounce blessings in his name."

Then He even made sure that His very words of blessings would be spoken, as Numbers 6:22–26 tells us:

> The LORD said to Moses, "Tell Aaron and his sons, 'This is how you are to bless the Israelites. Say to them: "The LORD bless you and keep you; the LORD make his face shine upon you and be gracious to you; the LORD turn his face toward you and give you peace."'"

Can you imagine what an honor it must have been for Aaron to stand and publicly proclaim God's blessing to all of Israel that first time? Imagine what it was like, knowing that God had given him the privilege of speaking God's very words to so many people. Consider the joy that swept over the Israelites as they heard these words spoken to them, knowing that they came directly from God and that He was expressing that He wanted to bless and keep them and also impart His favor, grace, and peace upon them.

Take note of this "generational" gift. When God appointed Aaron as the first high priest, every one of his descendants thereafter was born to the priesthood. By virtue of their bloodline they automatically had great privilege bestowed upon them.

In the New Testament, our relationship with Christ is actually defined as a blessing: "Praise be to the God and Father of our Lord Jesus Christ, who has blessed us in the heavenly realms with every spiritual blessing in Christ" (Ephesians 1:3). Dad, when you choose to echo those blessings in the life of one of God's precious daughters, God partners with you to dramatically transform this young lady's heart.

The Privilege

At this moment, I [Doreen] pray that you are struck with awe, knowing that you hold the position of the high priest of your household and have the privilege of blessing all those in your sphere of influence.

I hope joy and anticipation will sweep over your mind and heart as you prepare to create a blessing for your daughter. I encourage you first to use your chief privilege—your direct access to God—prayer! Ask Him to give you the words that He wants to speak through you, using your creative mind and sincere heart to bless your daughter.

Dr. Gary Smalley and Dr. John Trent, authors of the *The Blessing*, created a very simple format on how to impart a blessing upon our children (this format can be used to bless your spouse and others, as well). I am quite confident that this book has impacted thousands, if not millions, of lives since its first publication over 25 years ago!

I have seen hundreds of blessings imparted over the years and I can honestly say that every man who has asked God to speak through him (acting as the priest he has been called to be), has powerfully imparted the blessing which that young lady yearned to hear!

Please refer to the Appendix for the simplified format taken from the *The Blessing*. This is a great guideline for every father or father representative who is preparing a blessing. As you review the worksheet, you will see the importance of attaching high value through a word picture. Note that throughout the Bible God communicates through word pictures. For example:

> Like a roaring lion or a charging bear is a wicked man ruling over a helpless people. (Proverbs 28:15)
>
> Even youths grow tired and weary, and young men stumble and fall; but those who hope in the LORD will renew their strength. They will soar on wings like eagles; they will run and not grow weary, they will walk and not be faint. (Isaiah 40:30–31)
>
> My son, if you accept my words and store up my commands within you . . . applying your heart to understanding . . . if you look for it as for silver and search for it as for hidden treasure, then you will understand the fear of the LORD and find the knowledge of God. (Proverbs 2:1–5)

Doesn't the picture empower the statement? God created a picture because He wants us to visualize His thoughts so we will remember them. Media today is all about visual effects. Commercials hope to create a picture you won't forget so you will want to eat it, drive it, wear it, and ultimately, buy it!

The best communicators today have learned this principle. Society is using the media to deliver "the picture" of what they want us to hear and believe! Let us learn to become God's best communicators and create pictures that will last forever in the minds of our children and those we love.

In order to further assist dads and other chosen men in preparation for creating this blessing, I give daughters the "My Favorites" worksheet, contained in the Appendix. This provides simple yet very significant information to help you prepare a personal blessing just for her. Whether you're blessing your daughter in a formal ceremony or speaking from the heart over a special dinner date, these favorites will help you create a word picture, which is the key to the most memorable way to remember any spoken word.

> *Be prepared for an emotional experience as you realize how your daughter has grown into a woman; she is no longer a "little girl."*
>
> —PASTOR RICK HATA, CHINESE COMMUNITY CHURCH, TORRANCE, CA

Samples of Fathers' Blessings

Eric's Blessing upon Laura

I am so excited and consider it a privilege to give this blessing to you, Laura.

I saw on your worksheet that you listed a wild horse as your favorite animal. I see you like a beautiful horse. But not a wild horse, because they have a very fiery disposition and are self-seeking. I see your disposition as beautiful, tempered, controlled, a being with restraint that serves others—like a horse that has become tamed and trained.

As I have watched you grow in the Lord and get the Lord's perspective on things, His wisdom has given you that restraint, self-discipline. I see that you like to run free at other times and how you have been endowed with grace.

You have a strong, instinctive ability to think and figure things out. It would be difficult for you to explain how you arrived at it so easily. That, too, is like a horse—I guess you could say you have "good horse sense."

There are things that are not horse-like but are also beautiful about you. You have such a heart to help others. You also have a peace within you that I pray will flow to others. Lastly, you are an affectionate person and have a strong sense of humor—you are a joy to our family.

Laura, your future is hidden in the Lord. I believe you will contribute to His glorious Kingdom by your faith and spiritual insight.

Lord, keep her in Your peace, grace, and confidence in You.

—Eric B.

Eric also shares with us, "I felt a great responsibility to speak forth God's blessing. I felt like this was a good opportunity to consider Laura's many precious traits that the Lord had created within her. Since her Night of Celebration, I have a strengthened desire to project the positives that I see in her and try to undo any negatives that I have projected upon her due to my lack of allowing God's grace to work in me."

Jeff's Blessing upon Ashley

Ashley, you were born with a beautiful smile. From when we first brought you home from the hospital until now, that smile still brings us joy.

I see you as a leader. You're an example to your younger brother and sister. Don't expect to be perfect. I just want you to know where to turn when life is hard—to us, your family.

When I was a child, my grandparents gave me a strong Christian foundation. Today I want to give back into your life what was given to me. I hope when you are 39 years old and you have your own children, you will pass the same unto them.

I want to share with you Matthew 7:24 where Jesus said, "Everyone who hears these words of mine and puts them into practice is like a wise man who built his house on the rock."

Jeff further shares with us:

My daughter Ashley has been through many ups and down with me. I had struggled with a drug addiction up until three years ago. Had this occasion been during that time, I would not have been given this opportunity to bless her. I felt so honored when she asked me. I thought she must have been making a mistake. How could a person like me bless such a beautiful child of God like her?

I believe the thing that impacted me most that night was just being able to be there as her father. I felt an enormous amount of peace go through me when I saw Ashley enter the room and walk down the aisle. I think one thing that fathers struggle with most is seeing their daughters becoming young ladies. Ashley's celebration has taken that fear away for me and I have been able to put her in God's hands.

—Jeff S.

P.S. I have not lived with my wife and children since 1995 because of my past drug addiction. However, now having been sober for 3 years and having gotten my life right with the Lord, we have reconciled and have just purchased our first home. We are looking forward to being a family once again.

Pete's Blessing upon Brittany

Brittany, when God knitted you in your mother's womb He was in a very imaginative mood. He has given you many gifts. What impresses me with the gifts God has given you is what you've done with your gifts. You have used those gifts to bless others and not used them exclusively on yourself. I know it is pleasing to God.

You are creative, compassionate, and loving. Most of all, your sense of humor takes away some of the burdens of life. You have an incomparable ability to live above life's hardships. You can brighten any situation in life because you are playful and a breath of fresh air.

Your favorite thing in nature is the rain. And your favorite song is "Singing in the Rain." That is just like you, your gift to live above life's storms. You are like what my uncle often said: "An answer looking for a question."

Let Christ continue to mold your character. You will continue to succeed as you put God first.

—Pete B.

Now that you have read a few blessings, let's give you some tips on writing your own for your Modern-Day Princess:
- Use the "My Favorites" sheet your daughter (or the young lady you are going to bless) filled out. Highlight words or phrases on it that stand out to you.

- Create your own "favorites" sheet about your daughter:
    - ~ What are your favorite traits of hers?
    - ~ What are your favorite memories of her?
    - ~ What are the talents, skills, or attributes of hers you most value or admire?
    - ~ What is a favorite "inside joke" or memory you two share?
    - ~ What is a favorite verse she has or you think describes her?
- Pray. Ask God to guide your thoughts and words.
- Write a rough draft. Read it aloud to hear how it sounds and to check the length. Make any changes. Read it aloud again.

If you want, practice reading the blessing in front of your pastor or another dad—keep it a secret from your daughter for maximum impact! You and your wife can decide if you want her to also be surprised on celebration night too! If your wife would like to hear it ahead of time, don't worry, she will still be touched that night—and every time in years to come that she thinks of, hears, or recalls your blessing. There is nothing more romantic than a great dad! You will win two hearts with this blessing, Dad—your daughter's and your wife's!

Lives will change because of your blessing: your daughter's, your family's, and mostly, yours.

For the Men Who Will Become
Fathers to the Fatherless

We would like to take this opportunity to address and encourage various individuals who will be asked to participate in a young girl's rite of passage other than her parents. We hope you will be able to see the important role that you will play. To some of the men reading this chapter, you will be called on to become a step-in dad. God's Word encourages this unique role.

In fact, throughout God's Word, it is evident that God foresaw that there would be a need for some to step in to become fathers to the father-less. God mentions this subject at least nine occasions in His Word. Obvi-ously this is important to Him!

In Deuteronomy 14:27–29 God commanded the Israelites not to neglect those living among them that were "aliens, the fatherless and the widows who live[d] in [their] towns." Listen to the promise God gave the Israelites if they would be obedient: "So that the LORD your God may bless you in all the work of your hands."

You may be an uncle, grandfather, godfather, pastor, youth pastor, teacher, cousin, or close family friend. What an honor for you to have been asked to fill the shoes of an absent father (regardless of whether his absence is by choice or circumstance)! While fathers are called to reflect the love of the Heavenly Father, you have been called to be like Christ— a gift given by God to impart His love to those who are fatherless.

Who Will Step Up?

As I [Doreen] mentioned earlier, two of the girls in my first class did not have fathers who were available for the blessing. One girl's father had com-mitted suicide just the year prior to her attending the class. The other had a father who took no interest in her or her sister, even though he lived just miles away.

I sought the Lord in prayer because I thought it might be too diffi-cult for each of these girls (or any girls like them who took this journey in the future) to find a man in her life, other than her father, who would be willing to impart her blessing. I questioned whether she would be able to find a man that she respected enough to ask and who would care enough to embrace that honor.

As I set my concern before the Lord, Jeremiah 32:27 (KJV) came to mind. "Behold, I am the LORD, the God of all flesh: is there any thing too hard for me?"

How could I argue with God and His Word? I got up from that prayer time knowing that God would be faithful to provide a man to impart a blessing on any young girl who chose to take this journey in her life.

Since that time, I have taken hundreds of girls through the Modern-Day Princess rite of passage and over one-third of those girls have not had a father available to bless them. However, not one of those precious young girls has been left without a significant man to bless her. I have seen many men take on the challenging opportunity. God, as He has promised, is faithful to raise up fathers for the fatherless.

The young girl whose father had committed suicide and the other girl who had an absent father both asked our youth pastor. He was so honored by their asking him that he wept when he came to ask me how he should impart a blessing. On the night of their celebration, he appropriately demonstrated a genuine love and pronounced a wonderful affirmation to both of them. This was so needed during this season of their lives.

When someone steps up to become a father to the fatherless, he can be confident that he, too, will be blessed.

Stand in by You . . . Step Up for Her

If you wonder if being a "step-in" dad makes a real, long-term difference in a young woman's life, consider my own example. I [Pam] had an earthly father who loved me, but his own dysfunction and alcoholism kept him from ever really imparting a blessing. He never read my writing, came to my speaking events, or showed much interest in my talents. Even as a newlywed, that pain was still there in my heart.

Then Jim and Sally Conway, best-selling authors and professors of ours in seminary, offered to mentor Bill and me. One day, when Jim heard the pain in my life over the lack of blessing from my biological dad, he said, "Pam, I believe in you. I believe you are gifted, talented, and that you are a godly woman God will greatly use and bless. When you feel you need a dad, remember, I will be your dad. I am proud of you."

Jim's blessing freed me to enjoy and live out the calling on my life in a unique way. Both Bill and I are forever grateful for Jim and Sally and their blessing over our lives.

My continued prayer is that every young girl will have the opportunity to experience a meaningful rite of passage and have her father, or another significant man in her life, impart a blessing upon her. And that the man who says "yes" to the request will experience the joy and the blessing that God will return upon him because of his obedience to God's call.

Tips on Writing a Blessing as a Step-In Dad

As a step-in dad, there are a few extra things to keep in mind before you write the blessing:

- Be sure that you have a copy of the "My Favorites" sheet from your young lady. If you do not yet have one, make a copy from the Appendix and have her fill that out for you.
- Speak privately or make a phone call to her mother. Ask her what personality or character traits she appreciates in her daughter.

- Speak with others who may know her more personally, asking the same of them (what they love or appreciate about her).
- Pray that the Lord will give you wisdom and insight as you put your thoughts on paper.
- Find out if her dad is somewhere in the picture (e.g., a military man on foreign assignment, an out-of-state dad due to divorce, or maybe someone not willing to do this because he isn't a Christian). If it is appropriate for you to do so, call him and have him provide you with his thoughts about his daughter and be sure to include those in your blessing. (Please use wisdom and discretion and obtain the mother's approval before you proceed with contacting a father.)

Let me reassure you that as you pray and prepare her blessing, God will give you all you need to make it powerful and meaningful to her and to you!

Let's take a look at a few examples of what this has looked like in the past.

Courtney's Story

Courtney was 14 years old, full of life, and loved to talk. However, as she sat across from me that night, tears rolled down her cheeks as she told me: "I met my parents for the first time last summer. They were both 16 when I was born so I was put into foster care. I tried to kill myself twice before I was 7 years old because I hated the home I was living in. My grandmother was able to get custody of me and I've been with her ever since. My dad is a drug addict and may be going to jail for the next year and I don't know him that well anyway."

My [Doreen's] heart was filled with compassion and my eyes filled with tears as I feared that my next question might cause her more pain. However, we were down to the last week before the Celebration and she had not yet told me whom she had chosen to impart her blessing. I was praying that she had someone! I found the words falling out of my mouth, "Cookie (her nickname), who have you chosen to impart your blessing?"

Suddenly a smile warmed her face. "My godfather. He is a man I've known a couple of years. He talks about God and the Bible while he's teaching me how to ride and care for horses. I've already asked him and he has said yes."

At that moment I believe I was more thrilled than Courtney, but refrained from leaping with joy and just hugged her, stating that I would call and talk with him the following day. I spoke with her godfather, Willie, the following morning. As we spoke, he was quite excited about an opportunity to do something special for Courtney. I faxed him the necessary information, as her Celebration was just three days away.

The night of the rehearsal I saw a large, muscular Samoan man move toward the front. I approached him and learned that he was Courtney's godfather. He beamed with joy as he expressed what an honor he felt he had been given in doing this for her.

The evening of the celebration, he stood proudly as she walked down the aisle and slipped in next to him. Her small frame made her look like a tiny sprig next to a massive oak tree!

Soon I was introducing them as they headed to the platform. They came forward, one standing to one side of the microphone and one on the other.

Willie began sharing, "Courtney, I have three grown daughters, but never have I had the privilege with them that I am experiencing with you today." He then burst into tears and knocked over the microphone as he swept her into his arms. I couldn't see anything but Cookie's little feet momentarily as she was lost in his embrace. I don't believe there was a dry eye in the house, including her grandmother and her birth mother, who were both present that day.

His touching blessing incorporated Courtney's love for horses. Just imagine what this man's public affirmation did in the life of this 14-year-old girl! This is truly what it means to be a step-in dad for the young woman in your life.

Sydney's Story

Sydney was a young girl I [Doreen] had seen in our church when I implemented the first DOK class. She raced through doors and rooms like a Tasmanian devil. Two years later, Sydney joined the largest Modern-Day Princess group I've led since its inception. I knew that Sydney's grandparents were raising her, and other Christian friends from her community and our church had befriended her. When it was time for her to choose who would impart her blessing, Sydney chose her youth leader, Kenny.

The night of her celebration, he began to share how she had stated that her favorite animal was a monkey. The crowded laughed heartily, knowing this young lady. Kenny continued after the laughter died down:

> I took the time to go to the zoo this week, just to observe the monkeys so I could accurately apply their ways to your life. I found that:
> - They stick together as family—just like you, your brother, and grandparents. AND
> - They care for each other by picking off each other's fleas and parasites (laughter!)—that reminded me of how you and your friends care about each other.

• Most of all they are fun-loving, swinging from the trees,
back and forth, and chattering all the time—just like you,
Sydney!

He then shared how he had seen her growth over the last few years
from an out-of-control little girl to a mature young lady.

Then, as he placed her tiara upon her head, I believe I saw an immediate increase of self-respect in her eyes. He had bestowed her with honor
in the midst of some rich laughter!

Sample of a Step-In Dad's Blessings

Cindy's Blessing by Her Uncle

Cindy, you and I have had a bond between us since you were
born. We have been through some good times and some bad
times. Our bond has brought us together as friends as well as
relatives.

You said your favorite roses were red and white. I see the
white rose representing your innocence and the red rose representing the loving person you are.

You said that your favorite animal was a dolphin. As I
thought about that, I saw how you are like them. They are caring,
friendly, free, and graceful. Wow! That was the first time I saw
how you are just like them—that's your name!

You have many good characteristics and I could take hours to
express how special you are. I know your future holds all God has
for you because your devotion is toward Him. I'll always be there
for you.

—Uncle Luke

Dad (or step-in dad), become a man that blesses. Nothing is more masculine than a man who recognizes the power of his words and uses that power to protect and provide a future for a young girl's life.

Mentor Moment

Whether you are a dad or a step-in dad, you are in a role of influence, a male mentor so to speak. Proverbs 6:20–23 (MSG) sheds light on the power of your role:

> Good friend, follow your father's good advice; don't wander off from your mother's teachings. Wrap yourself in them from head to foot; wear them like a scarf around your neck. Wherever you walk, they'll guide you; whenever you rest, they'll guard you; when you wake up, they'll tell you what's next. For sound advice is a beacon, good teaching is a light, moral discipline is a life path.

While words of blessing are powerful, there is another, incredible gift you can also give this young lady: *your presence.*

The editor for this book shared a moving story over lunch that displayed the power of a father's presence. Her first year out of high school, she attended a college with an intense discipleship program. After she had been there several months, she became uneasy with some of the practices, requirements, and theologies of the program. She struggled with her desire to leave, because she had agreed with her parents that she would stay for at least one semester. Her agreement with her parents, and her fear of being thought of as a failure, kept her from withdrawing from the school.

Early in her second semester, however, she realized that she would never be comfortable with the college's practices and theology. She prayed for weeks over her decision, and finally felt God's release and peace to leave. She called her parents, still afraid that they might be disappointed in her decision not to fully complete the program. But they immediately agreed to drive the three hours necessary to pick her up.

It was understood at this place that if someone chose to withdraw, no one should help that person pack or carry luggage out of the dormitory. Repeatedly she had to walk back and forth through the hallways, carrying her possessions to the front door.

With a heavy heart, she saw her parents drive up and went to retrieve her last suitcase. But as she reached the front door, she saw something that made all the difference. Her dad was standing on the steps, holding out a simple red rose to her. He wrapped his arms around her and said three simple words, "I love you." She knew without reservations she was safe, at home, accepted, and everything was going to be all right again.

That is the power of a father's presence. This young woman in your life is counting on you to "be there." Even if you do not have immediate answers or solutions, your presence alone is a comfort.

Ask yourself:

- Am I "there" for my daughter? (or the young woman in your life)
- Am I listening to her?
- Do I ask about her day, her friends, her fears, her joys?
- Am I "checked in" when I get home from work or am I preoccupied with my own list of priorities and desires?
- Do I attend her activities?

For men becoming step-in dads, when you give a blessing to a Modern-Day Princess, your role is a bit different. Simply ask yourself, "In my role (as uncle, brother, coach, pastor, etc.), do I show genuine, appropriate concern for this girl?" You can't be her father, but you can play the best possible role of a man of integrity in her life.

Your Patience

Teen girls are impossible, irrational, and irritating at times. Raging hormones and emotional turbulence is par for the course. You don't need to give in to her demands or whims, but you do need to be engaged and alert to them so you can help her through them.

Ask yourself:

- Am I calm when my daughter is on an emotional merry-go-round?

• Am I using words that edify instead of reacting to
  her?
• Am I seeking to help her problem-solve and move to
  a more peaceful place?

For the step-in dad simply ask: Am I being a role model of care and concern, and a man who is not easily ruffled and angered?

Your Paycheck

Just hand it over. Just kidding! But we are pretty sure that is how you might feel at times. Women, especially young women, observe your attitude toward spending money on them. Dads who fund the lavish, over-the-top, Sweet 16 parties as seen on TV are asking for trouble. You might be creating a consumer monster that no other man will ever be able to satisfy. Your precious, pampered princess might conclude that love is expressed through your credit cards, bank accounts, and unlimited budgets, which will set her up for marital distress in the future.

On the other hand, your daughter will feel rejected if you cannot find a way to somehow celebrate her. It doesn't have to be lavish or expensive, but it does need to be acknowledged. If you roll your eyes, sigh, or complain when you are asked for money at her most important moments of life, she will feel you do not care about her. If money is tight, brainstorm with her on ways to help her help fund what matters to her. She will still sense you care if you work with her to mark a moment or reach a goal.

Your Personal Integrity

More than anything, your character counts. If you say "I love you," but then risk her life by driving drunk or smoking with her in the car or home, she will soon figure out that your vices are more important than her.

If you say "I love you," but you cheat on her mom, delve into pornography, or walk away from the family, she will assume you think your personal happiness is more important than her.

If you say "I love you," then break the law or break a promise in a way her reputation or social structure is eroded, she will surmise that your words have no meaning because your choices have put all that she values at risk.

For the step-in dad, simply ask: Is my inner life matching this outer blessing I am about to give?

The best blessing you can give is to back up your words with a life of integrity. Bless her with your character!

Final Words to the Adults Who Love These Modern-Day Princesses

For you must teach others those things you and many others
have heard me speak about. Teach these great truths to trustworthy men [and women] who will, in turn, pass them on to others.

—2 Timothy 2:2 (TLB)

Without faith, nothing is possible. With it,
nothing is impossible.

—Mary McLeod Bethune

As you've seen through the stories and examples throughout this book, you have the potential to unlock the future for one young woman—or many of them. You are the caring adult God has placed in her world. We wanted to take time to answer some of your questions and concerns so that you have all you need to now move forward and bless the girls in your realm of influence.

For Church and Community Leaders

As a leader within a church or community organization, you hold the key to your city or region. Your support of a rite-of-passage program, such as Becoming a Modern-Day Princess, can be the difference between success and failure of the groups that could begin in your church. The rite-of-passage preparation and celebration will help disciple young women who can reach the tween and teen girls and families of your community, many who might never hear or know of the love of God any other way.

Pam's husband, Bill, was a youth pastor for 8 years and then served as a senior pastor for more than 15. Most recently, he served as a small-group pastor under Dr. David Jeremiah while ministering to couples and families through the Farrels' parachurch ministry. We asked Bill to join us [Pam and Doreen] as we lay out for you 10 reasons why a rite of passage is a good idea:

Women Need It: Women fill counseling offices. Anything a church or organization can do to prevent or correct a pain in a young girl's heart or dysfunction in her home of origin will lower your counseling load, as well as protect each girl from poor choices made out of a broken heart. One needs only look at the sheer number of adult women in pain to conclude that many of these women could have greatly benefited from hearing her father's blessing during those critical teen years. Far more might also tell you that if they had received the vital training, equipping, and encouragement in making wise, healthy choices during their teen years, life might have turned out differently for them.

Dads Want It: Many dads want to help their daughters but need some help doing it. Most fathers want to do the right thing but often are not well equipped to create a moment as meaningful as a rite-of-passage celebration on their own. The blessing of the rite-of-passage ceremony helps a dad know how to say what he longs to say to his daughter and provides him a comfortable and appropriate setting in which to do it.

In addition, fathers long for appropriate ways to connect and express affection to their tween and teen daughters. Rite-of-passage celebrations provide a positive opportunity to do just that. Daughters will also gain an appreciation for their fathers and see Dad as more than an ATM, or a disciplinarian, or the guy in the chair watching football. When Dad places that crown on her head and she hears words of blessing from him, he becomes the most important man in her life, next to Jesus.

Moms Long For It: Mothers are wonderful cheerleaders for their daughters, and a rite of passage provides the structure yet fun opportunity many moms wish they had had as a girl. Mothers, more than any other person in a girl's life, know the importance of marking the memorable moments on the journey into womanhood. Being a woman can be a complicated role in today's world, and any way we can help Mom educate and inspire her daughter is a worthy goal. The happy memories of heart-to-heart discussions, picking out a special dress, learning to use makeup and manners, and praying for one another can greatly deepen the mother/daughter bond.

In addition, if Mom also becomes the mentor to a group of Modern-Day Princesses, a daughter can look to her mother's leadership example and role model as one to emulate.

Girls Love It: The girls themselves enjoy it. If a small group is formed, it becomes a way to make long-lasting, godly friends. The things learned during the rite-of-passage journey can deter the petty, unproductive, mean-spirited relationship issues that sometimes crop up in the teen years in a girl's life.

Young women also feel more secure and confident as they learn to care for others, to recognize what a godly woman looks, acts, and dresses like, and to make wise choices in friendships and future guy/girl relationships. Finally, it equips a young woman to have a vital, growing relationship with God, and to embrace her identity in Christ and walk in a manner worthy of her royal standing.

Communities Crave It: A consistent, widespread use of a rite-of-passage program can dramatically impact a community. As young women begin to recognize their value and worth and families are drawn into the local church, the rates of premarital sex, teen pregnancy, abortion, prostitution, drugs, drinking, and all kinds of social problems have the possibility of lowering. In a community that fully embraces a rite-of-passage program for teen girls, the entire teen culture of junior and senior high schools can be positively affected.

Families Desire It: The average family is filled with well-meaning but very busy people. A rite of passage provides a simple, easy-to-use program that is both personal yet reproducible. The entire extended family can be pulled in to participate in the celebration: older sisters, moms, aunts, and grandmothers can serve as mentors and encouragers; Dad as the giver of the blessing; and brothers, grandfathers, and uncles as Modern-Day Knights serving to make the evening run smoothly behind the scenes. Memories will be made and relationships enhanced as the family gathers around the princess at this special moment.

Leaders Appreciate It: Directors of women's ministries and youth pastors see the value of a rite of passage as these girls grow into the young women leaders who take over leadership. Often, church leaders are looking for discipleship programs they can believe in yet easily implement in their busy schedules.

In addition, a church that sponsors rite-of-passage programs, celebrations, and/or conferences will be seen in the community as a church that cares for and equips youth. Additionally, with a large percentage of youth walking away from their faith in their college and early adult years, churches must come alongside our young men and women and offer support and instruction. And for a teen girl preparing to go to college, her heart will likely remain invested in the church home that chose to invest in her.

School Teachers Compliment It: A rite of passage helps create more young ladies who are easier to teach and eager to learn. Teachers yearn for students who are positive, have great relationship skills, and are good mediators in and outside the classroom, and through a rite of passage, young women can become more confident, more appreciative, and more eager to seek out and develop opportunities to learn and grow.

Community Leaders Adapt It: A motivated leader can take biblically based truths and move them into the public arena where they are most needed. In addition, community groups that proactively mentor and equip youth will be seen by leaders and community members as organizations to invest in and participate in. These organizations may be strengthened by a renewed enthusiasm that can result from implementing a rite-of-passage program or by offering families the setting in which to host a rite-of-passage celebration.

God Anoints It: Because the Becoming a Modern-Day Princess concept is a biblically based program with Scripture and scriptural principles woven throughout, God can place His hand of favor over the program and process. God implemented the blessing process so, of course, He would smile on it as it is used in this modern-day context.

For the Modern-Day Princess Facilitator

You might be a mom or a mentor or an alumna of the Modern-Day Princess program, but you are a woman with a heart to begin a Modern-Day Princess group.

We thought you might want to hear from other facilitators and leaders who have run groups. Some have run multiple groups year after year because they are enthusiastically enjoying watching young women's lives change for the better.

Here's what leaders are saying about the rite-of-passage process:

Holly is the wife of one of the men who helped found the Promise Keepers movement for men. She's also an MDP facilitator. Her favorite part of the Modern-Day Princess program is "watching the girls' faces when they are being honored by their fathers, and receive their crowns. Priceless . . . absolutely priceless."

Recently, Holly ran into one of her Modern-Day Princess graduates when she traveled back to one of the communities she had lived in and facilitated a group in the past. She noticed the change:

> This girl's whole countenance and demeanor was so foreign, in a positive way, that I honestly did not recognize her! When I was leading her, she was a new believer, very troubled due to a terrible home life, and she was at risk. Her father had been a very sketchy part of her life, but he did participate in the celebration. His presence there was significant.
>
> Now, she is settled, not trying to impress, walking with the Lord, and has a confidence about her that was simply not a part of her makeup prior to DOK (Daughters of the King). I could tell she felt comfortable with me, wasn't trying too hard, and she was just a pleasure to be around. I was amazed, and pleasantly shocked!

Kara is also a leader who is passionate about helping young women find their identity in Christ. She's seen positive changes in her own life as she has stepped out to lead:

> I have more confidence! It's something I always seek to instill in the girls, but it's something that I see growing in ME, too. I also watch the example I set before the girls very closely. I'm more

aware of the way I carry myself and aware of the decisions I make. My walk with the Lord is more consistent and I have a deeper love relationship with Him because of the program. If I believe what we teach the girls—that Jesus is passionate about them, forgiving everything, loving them completely, and wanting to be a part of everything they do—I want to live that out in my life, too. I live more deliberately, intentionally, and with much more JOY!

Julie is a mother who originally participated with the DOK program for her own daughter and now is the Canadian Representative for the MDP program across Canada. Even though Julie is a mature, seasoned leader, she has sensed growth in her life as a result of being a part of the Modern-Day Princess program:

> By leading this study, it has encouraged me to continually face my own life as a woman and the lies I sometimes still get caught up in. The biggest ones relate to self-esteem, self-worth, and self-centeredness. One of the key phrases I use while teaching this study is, "Life is not always about you, so get over yourself." God desires us to have a heart to love and serve others and this study constantly reminds me not to think higher of myself than I ought.

For Moms and Dads

We know that implementing a rite-of-passage ceremony or family celebration often comes down to Mom and Dad. Frequently you are the ones to plan, coordinate, and fund what matters most to your daughter—and this is no exception. Because of this, we thought you might appreciate it if we answered some frequently asked questions.

Do I need to do a whole program or can we just hold a family rite-of-passage celebration with our immediate family? Truly, each piece of the Raising a Modern-Day Princess process should be seen as a building block. Your family can decide to use many of the building blocks or just a few. Each and every piece will build into your daughter's life, but you should feel free to mix and match the building blocks and adapt, mold, and morph the pieces to best suit your family's personality, your daughter's personality, and your own family traditions and budget.

How much will this cost? To implement a program such as MDP, the cost ranges from well under $50 to approximately $175 (depending on how elaborate you want the rite-of-passage celebration to be and if the celebration is shared with other families or a family-based celebration where your own extended family is invited). For example: $100 per girl would break down to:

- $12 for her journal
- $10 refreshments for weekly classes
- $10 miscellaneous items for classes such as cards, little gifts, etc.
- $20 for a beautiful tiara
- $10 for her bouquet
- $38 participation in celebration, possibly facility use cost, or items such as flowers

(The $100 price tag per girl can be greatly lowered if parents, a church, or vendors in the community donate the essentials of the rite-of-passage ceremony.)

If you elect not to gather a group, but to do something more private as a rite of passage for your daughter, then the cost might be simply the price you paid for this book and any expenses Mom decides to spend throughout her daughter's rite-of-passage and celebration experience.

How much time will it take? The Modern-Day Princess program can be formatted in several different ways:

Weekly meetings with a rite-of-passage celebration at the end to which family and friends are invited. This can be private mentoring between Mom and daughter or done with a group of her friends (and their moms if they'd like to all participate).

A weekend retreat that the girls attend. The retreat might end on Sunday evening and at that time family and friends join the girls for the ceremony and celebration.

A weekend away for Mom and daughter to work their way through the Becoming a Modern-Day Princess material found in this book. This could end with meeting up with Dad or the family (and friends) for a personal rite-of-passage ceremony or celebration such as a party or a special dinner.

If a weekly program is attended, each class is normally an hour and a half to two hours. If it is a weekend retreat, it normally starts on a Friday evening and ends with the celebration on Sunday evening. But as we've said, you know your family system and schedule; adapt the material to best fit your needs.

My daughter has been raised in a strong Christian home. How can she benefit? Holly (the facilitator we mentioned earlier) sees the most influential part of the MDP program for girls from strong Christian homes is their ability to learn how to step out from their comfortable friendship cliques, usually with other girls from Christian homes, and reach out to others who might be newer to the faith or from homes that need the love of Christ. As she says, "It was satisfying to see girls become more like Christ by putting away what made them comfortable . . . and going out of their way to be others-centered."

How do we get started? Since every princess needs a crown, let's use the acrostic C.R.O.W.N. to describe the steps to take to implement a rite-of-passage experience for your daughter or the young tween and teen girls under your realm of influence:

Create a Plan
Rally Help
Offer Opportunity
Work with Dad
Notice the Princess

Create a Plan

Decide what kind of rite-of-passage experience you want to offer your daughter or the girls in your sphere of influence. Pray, talk over the options and the budget with your spouse if you are married, run the idea by your daughter and get her input, and then make the decision that best reflects your family's desires and needs. Create a plan that best suits your daughter and the future God is preparing for her.

Rally Help

If you are a mother or a woman who has a heart to become a future MDP facilitator and you desire to see a group rite of passage implemented in your church, school, or local youth organization, we would suggest that you share your passion with the leadership of your church or organization. Then offer your help and possibly give the leadership of that particular institution a copy of this book. (You might also consider providing them the *Becoming a Modern-Day Princess Promotional DVD* that is available by contacting www.treasuredcelebrations.org.) When you get the green light to move forward, start contacting the moms of teenage girls in your area to spread the word and begin recruiting help.

If you choose to implement the Becoming a Modern-Day Princess program, you might decide to have a few copies of the *Raising a Modern-Day Princess* book on hand at that initial "interest" meeting, and maybe a princess's journal, so moms can see what their teen daughter will experience. This is also a service to the busy mom who might have trouble making it to a bookstore. (You can also just have one of each and take orders as girls are registered, or provide ordering information to the moms and allow each family to be responsible for having the book and journal in hand by a preset start date.)

Also if you're using the program, plan on sharing copies of *Becoming a Modern-Day Princess Promotional DVD* or show the online clip. Ask for help from the parents at the informational meeting. You might be pleasantly surprised by the support of your efforts to get it started. If you have a sign-up sheet for volunteer needs and registration cards, most mothers will sign their daughters up and volunteer on the spot!

Once you have a group of girls committed to attend, determine the meeting location(s), order your leadership guide and girls journals, and you will soon be on your way to experiencing the joy of seeing your group of girls become Modern-Day Princesses!

You may want to have the date of the rite-of-passage ceremony set on the first day of the Modern-Day Princess meeting so the girls and the parents have something to look forward to from the very beginning. The date of the rite-of-passage ceremony can also be shared with the parents at the "interest meeting" so that busy families can set aside the date and you can recruit help for the big event.

Do not be discouraged by the various details that must be handled. Parents are usually excited and enthused to help with such an exciting life-changing event for their daughter! (You can also have two meetings, one just to see what interest might be in your daughter's friendship circle or youth group and a second to work out the details and recruit for the program elements and the celebration and ceremony.)

Blessing a Modern-Day Princess is God's great idea so His power and provision will be with you as you move forward in this process!

Offer Opportunity

After you know the plan and have some help, now it's time to offer your daughter, or her friends, or the girls in the youth group or nearby community, the option of taking part in this rite of passage. We encourage you to make the invitation personal, pretty, and full of promise.

Personal: Approach your daughter one-on-one first, even if she will be going to a meeting to learn more details. Show her you value her individuality, her opinions, and her input.

Pretty: Make the invitation special. It can be on a pretty note card, or accompanied with a cute little gift (like a crown key chain), or given over a beautifully set table with her favorite meal or tea.

Promise: Explain to her why you believe this is a great opportunity for her and describe some of the things she will experience and learn as a result. Lay out for her how this will benefit her in the long run, but also include how much she will have fun doing it in the present!

Work with Dad

Once the plan is set, begin working with Dad (or dads), and give him (or them) plenty of time to prepare the blessing. If you're working with a group, you might invite all the dads to coffee and ask a male leader (a pastor or community leader with a daughter) to join you and give the men the tools to use for creating the blessing and make sure they have time to meet the other dads with daughters. The fathers might end up encouraging one another further down the line.

Notice the Princess

Once a plan is in place, the princess is a priority. This is a unique window of time to build into her life so protect your time with your daughter (or the girls in the group). Allow plenty of time in your own schedule to give the mentoring, the planning, the discussions over the lessons, and the celebration the time they deserve to make this a very special memory for your princess. You might go ahead and designate a specific time each week to devote to your daughter's rite-of-passage experience.

If you focus well on your part of the process, soon she will be wearing her crown and even more importantly, she will be embracing her role and identity as a daughter of the King of Kings.

Mentor Moments

It is often a pain, a great pain, that provides the passion behind a big vision. You've heard that both Doreen and I [Pam] longed for our own biological father's blessing. In addition to this, through our ministries, we have each personally witnessed the devastation that can happen in a teen's life when the blessing is withheld, or worse, when a daughter feels rejected by her earthly father. One example stands out in our minds vividly and propels us forward in the vision of creating a world where every daughter gets a blessing by her own father or a step-in father.

We'll call this young girl Nena—and you might, right now, have a "Nena" in your world. She might be in your church, your neighborhood, or your apartment building. She could be your daughter's friend or her classmate. She could be a relative or the daughter of a friend. She needs hope. She needs to know *you* are there. Why does she need to know? Let's allow her story to show you:

> At the age of three, Nena's mommy and daddy divorced. Even though the marriage ended as a result of abuse, she hungered to have her daddy in her life. Mom remarried but this second man in her life had no interest in her, which heightened her desire to seek out her father.
>
> At the age of 10, after many petitions expressing her desire to see her father, Mom agreed. They were able to locate him and discovered that he had also remarried and now had two children under the age of five. The first time he and his family met with Nena and her mom, they all met in a neutral location. (Mom didn't want Dad to know where they lived.)
>
> It seemed like a positive encounter for this precious little girl who was so hungry to feel her daddy's love. There were several visits in the ensuing months, and all seemed well as she returned from each visit excitedly telling everyone she was part of their family. Then one day, Nena asked her father and his wife if she could come and live

with them and the answer was yes. He and his wife were willing to take her in.

She arrived in their home feeling like a part of this new family. She now had her daddy, a stepmother, and a younger brother and sister. She excelled in school even as she entered school mid-semester and ended the year with straight A's. Everyone was thrilled with her adjustment to the new family and school.

During that summer things begin heating up. Nena felt she saw evidence that the other two children were preferred over her. Soon she was watching the children often—like a built-in babysitter.

Nena, by nature, is an outspoken child. Thus, she whined about her new responsibility to her stepmother, who in turn told her father. After hearing this, he took her to her room and slapped her face for the disrespect she was showing toward his family.

It wasn't long before she called her mother, desperately begging to come home. Her mom called and spoke to the father and made arrangements to pick her up by the weekend. That evening Nena's father called and informed her mother that their daughter had snuck out of the house and couldn't be found. Two days passed and Mom got a knock on the door. Her 10-year-old girl had hitchhiked back home—more than one hundred miles. When she walked in the door, she told her mother that her father said, "If you leave this house, I'll never speak to you again." And he never has.

Upon her return home she began hanging with some of the neighborhood kids and you could see the hard edges of her character beginning to form. By the age of 11, she had falsely accused her mother of child-abuse and shortly thereafter ran away from home. By the time she was 13, she had been in and out of juvenile detention several times and was now pregnant by her pimp with her first child. By the time she was 17 years of age, she had three little girls and the grandparents took legal custody of all of them.

Several years ago she called her family, happily telling them she was pregnant and in love with a new man in her life. She was proud that she was taking methadone to help her get completely off heroin. She informed the family that her relationship was with a man who had served eight years in prison (but he was falsely accused) and was now out on parole for good behavior. They soon had a beautiful little girl.

Nena thought that after the baby was born, her boyfriend would never hit her again. But within three weeks of the baby coming home from the hospital, he beat her again. Nena called her family, screaming for help, and they called 911. The father of that baby was sent back to jail immediately and she was left to care for her new baby alone. She was angry with the family members who had made the 911 call and began blaming them for ruining her life.

Within weeks of this episode, Nena's aunt came over

one day to help her put curtains on the windows in her new home. When she walked into the home, she found Nena in the bathroom, washing a sheet that appeared to have blood on it. When Nena turned to look at her, her aunt saw a two-inch gaping hole in her neck—she could even see the carotid artery pulsating in the wound. Nena had attempted suicide.

Her aunt immediately called the family for help. Nena's cousin took the baby while her aunt rushed her to the emergency room. All of a sudden, while driving to the hospital, Nena's head started bobbing. She was losing consciousness.

They arrived at the county hospital and the doctors discovered that Nena had also overdosed on antidepressant drugs. She later admitted that she had taken over 30 pills.

Within days she was released into the custody of her family, along with the baby. She was now in a safe place to recover and bring order into her life. However, within weeks, one day she said she was going for a walk and never came back.

Randomly, she calls her family, but never reveals her location. Nena is now in her thirties. From what they can piece together, the baby was taken away from her and she is still addicted to drugs, which she pays for with her life of prostitution. She continues to be in jail or to end up in the hospital for yet another "injury" at the hand of yet another out-of-control male.

Recently, in a cryptic call, Nena said she was living with a man 22 years her elder, and "He is taking care of me."

It's so obvious, isn't it? She's still seeking a daddy—still hoping for the blessing but living a life far from blessed.

This story is true, unfortunately. And every day, around the world, pieces of this story are repeated in the lives of young women, but it doesn't have to be that way. You can stand in the gap to rescue and redeem precious young women before the hurt and pain is lodged into their hearts in a destructive way.

If you have an emotionally, spiritually, and socially healthy family, the princess in your home has been commissioned to be "a light unto the world." Your daughter is stronger, more confident, more secure, and more able to hold out a hand of help and hope because she knows she has a family whose love is her safety net. As you bless her, you send her into a successful, bright future.

Your love is a light to your daughter and to all the young women you might meet. Let your light shine.

Notes

Chapter 1

1. Gary Smalley and John Trent, *The Gift of the Blessing* (Nashville, TN: Thomas Nelson, Inc., 1993 Edition), 217.
2. Dr. Dave Currie (former director of Family Life Canada), "The Transfer of the Sacred Trust." Used by permission.
3. Kaiser Family Foundation, "U.S. Teen Sexuality," (January 2005), http://www.kff.org/youthhivstds/upload/U-S-Teen-Sexual-Activity-Fact-Sheet.pdf.
4. Ibid.
5. Ibid.
6. Guttmacher Institute, "Facts on American Teens' Sexual and Reproductive Health," (September 2006), http://www.gutt macher.org/pubs/fb_ATSRH.html.
7. Ibid.
8. U.S. Department of Justice, Girls Study Group (May 2008), http://www.ncjrs.gov/pdffiles1/ojjdp/218905.pdf.
9. Ibid.
10. Dallas Jackson, quoted in Pioneer Thinking, "Mean Girls: How to Combat Bullying," (November 7, 2005), http://www.pioneer thinking.com/ara-meangirls.html.
11. Patrick Huguenin, "With cyber bullying, girls gone wild gets a horrifying new meaning," (April 10, 2008), http://www.ny dailynews.com/lifestyle/2008/04/10/2008-04-10_with_cyber _bullying_girls_gone_wild_gets.html.

12. Pioneer Thinking, "Mean Girls: How to Combat Bullying," (November 7, 2005), http://www.pioneerthinking.com /ara-meangirls.html.

13. "Statistics—Adolescent Depression," http://www.about-teen-depression.com/depression-statistics.html.

14. "More Girls than Boys Trying Drugs for First Time-US[sic]," (February 9, 2006), http://www.redorbit.com/news/health /385488/more_girls_than_boys_trying_drugs_for_first _timeus/.

15. Ibid.

16. http://kidshealth.org/parent/emotions/behavior/suicide.html (last viewed June 9, 2009).

17. Tracy Clark-Flory, "America's Youth Turned Amateur Porn Stars?" (December 10, 2008), http://www.salon.com/mwt /broadsheet/2008/12/10/teens_sexting/.

Chapter 2

1. Dr. James Dobson, *What Wives Wish Their Husbands Knew About Women* (Carol Stream, IL: Tyndale House Publishers, Inc., 1975), 35.

2. This information was researched and documented from the following sites: www.edah.org and http://en.wikipedia.org/wiki /Bat_mitzvahs.

3. This information was researched and documented from the following sites: http://www.quinceanera-boutique.com /quinceaneratradition.htm and www.wikipedia.org/wiki /quinceanera.

4. Many thanks to Patricia West-Barker, who wrote the article "Kinaalda: A Navajo girl's coming of age celebration. Molding the future from the past," *Santa Fe New Mexican,* July 3, 2005. Used by permission.

5. Ibid.

Chapter 3

1. http://www.merriam-webster.com/thesaurus/keep

2. Personal story shared with Pam Farrel. Used by permission. (www.LaneJordan.com)

3. Shared in personal conversation (March 2009). Used by permission.

4. Story shared with Pam Farrel (December 2008). Used by permission.

5. Story shared with Pam Farrel (December 2008). Cindy McMenamin is also the author of *When Women Walk Alone: Finding Strength and Hope Through the Seasons of Life* (Harvest House Publishers, 2002). Used by permission.

6. Personal story shared with Pam Farrel (December 2008). Used by permission.

7. Ibid.

8. Personal story shared with Pam Farrel (December 2008). Used by permission.

9. Jill Savage and Pam Farrel, *Got Teens?* (Eugene, OR: Harvest House Publishers, 2005).

10. Linda Newton, *I Want Something Better than Jewels* (Anderson, IN: Warner Press, 2009). Used by permission. (www.linda newtonspeaks.com)

Chapter 5

1. Personal story shared with Pam Farrel (December 2008). Used by permission.
2. Personal story shared with Pam Farrel (December 2008). Used by permission.
3. Angela Thomas's review of *Here for You: Creating a Mother-Daughter Bond that Lasts a Lifetime*, http://www.shelovesgod.com/library/article.cfm?articleid=9419.
4. Story shared with Pam Farrel (December 2008). To be published in *I Want Something Better than Jewels* (Anderson, IN: Warner Press, 2009). Used by permission.
5. Ibid.
6. Personal story shared with Pam Farrel. Used by permission.

Chapter 6

1. Pam Farrel, *Woman of Influence* (Chicago: InterVarsity Press, 2006).
2. Ibid.

Chapter 7

1. Robert Lewis, *Raising a Modern-Day Knight* (Carol Stream, IL: Tyndale House Publishers, 1997), 15–16.
2. Pam Farrel, *Woman of Confidence* (Eugene, OR: Harvest House Publishers, 2009).

Chapter 8

1. As quoted in Robert Wolgemuth's *She Calls Me Daddy* (Carol Stream, IL: Tyndale House Publishers, 1996), 3.

Recommended Resources

Books

Angela Thomas, *Do You Think I'm Beautiful?* Nashville, TN: Thomas Nelson, Inc., 2005.

Bill and Pam Farrel, *The 10 Best Decisions a Woman Can Make.* Eugene, OR: Harvest House Publishers, 2004.

Bill and Pam Farrel, *The 10 Best Decisions Every Parent Can Make.* Eugene, OR: Harvest House Publishers, 2006.

Chad Eastham and Bill and Pam Farrel, *Guys Are Waffles, Girls Are Spaghetti.* Nashville, TN: Thomas Nelson, Inc., 2009.

Dave and Claudia Arp, *Suddenly They're 13.* Grand Rapids, MI: Zondervan, 1999.

Dr. Gary Smalley and Dr. John Trent, *The Blessing.* (Revised edition) Nashville, TN: Thomas Nelson, Inc., 2004.

Fern Nichols and Janet Kobobel Grant, *Every Child Needs a Praying Mom.* Grand Rapids, MI: Zondervan, 2003.

Jill Savage and Pam Farrel, *Got Teens?* Eugene, OR: Harvest House Publishers, 2005.

Jim and Suzette Brawner, *Taming the Family Zoo.* Longwood, FL: Xulon Press, 2007.

John and Kendra Smiley, *Be the Parent.* Chicago: Moody Publishers, 2006.

June Moore, *Manners Made Easy for Teens*, Nashville, TN: B&H Publishing Group, 2007.

Other

Doreen Hanna, founder of Treasured Celebrations, provides the *Becoming a Modern-Day Princess Journal* and *The Modern-Day Princess Group Leader's Guide* for youth leaders and mentors. Also available is a community-based *Today's Modern-Day Princess Leader's Guide* and *Today's Modern-Day Princess Journal.* For more information go to: www.treasuredcelebrations.org.

Dr. Gary Smalley and Dr. John Trent. "Blessing Others," a Focus on the Family broadcast. (CD283)

Randy and Lisa Wilson. "A Father's Commitment to Purity," a two-part Focus on the Family broadcast. (B01646D)

Dennis Rainey, "Interviewing Your Daughter's Date: 8 Steps to No Regrets." (Audio CD)

Bill and Pam Farrel, *Teen Relationship Contract.* (www.farrel communications.com)

Florence and Marita Littauer, *Wired That Way Personality Profile.*

www.emilypost.com (Resources for etiquette and table manners)

www.teen-beauty-tips.com (Lessons on natural beauty)

Note: Mary Kay cosmetics and their consultants are most often ready and willing to provide a makeover for moms and their teenage daughters. This is an excellent resource because they have a line of simple teen products.

Appendix

Family Legacy Worksheet

Fill in the blanks below and consider adding a word or two to describe each family member. For example, Maternal Grandmother—talented singer, kind; Father—quiet, hardworking. (Mom can help with those the daughter may not have known.) Feel free to leave blank those names that are unknown or insert other names that are known (e.g., Aunt, Uncle, First Cousin, etc.). Note: In a family tree such as this one, all women's names should be written in maiden form.

MY FAMILY TREE

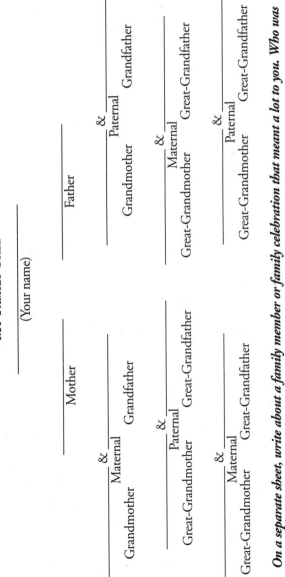

_____
(Your name)

_____ Mother

_____ Father

&
_____
Maternal
Grandmother

_____ Grandfather

&
_____
Paternal
Grandmother

_____ Grandfather

&
_____
Paternal
Great-Grandmother

_____ Great-Grandfather

&
_____
Maternal
Great-Grandmother

_____ Great-Grandfather

&
_____
Maternal
Great-Grandmother

_____ Great-Grandfather

&
_____
Paternal
Great-Grandmother

_____ Great-Grandfather

On a separate sheet, write about a family member or family celebration that meant a lot to you. Who was there?

Questions for Daughter to Ask Dad
(or Step-in Dad)

1. Recall for me some of the most important lessons you have learned in life.

2. Who was the first person to talk to you about God? What effect did this have on you?

3. When did you become a Christian? How did your life change?

4. Who gave you your first Bible? How old were you when you received it? How has it influenced your life?

5. What scent or sound immediately takes you back to your childhood? Describe the feeling it evokes.

6. Have you ever felt that God has a special calling on your life?

7. What was the hardest thing you ever had to do?

8. What meaningful advice have you received from an adult? What were the circumstances?

9. Share some insights from Scripture that have guided your spiritual journey.

10. Up to this point, what would you have done differently in life if you could?

11. What individuals have had the greatest impact in your life? How did they impact your life?

12. What advice would you like to pass on to your children, grandchildren, and great-grandchildren?

13. What have been the most important milestones or turning points in your life?

14. So far, what do you consider the greatest success of your life?

15. Who would you consider your closest friend? Why?

16. What family traditions would you most like to continue?

17. What prayers have you been praying for your children and grandchildren?

Six Statements of Forgiveness

(Adapted from *Love, Honor and Forgive* [InterVarsity Press] and *The 10 Best Decisions a Woman Can Make* [Harvest House] by Bill and Pam Farrel)

For use by girls who feel they need to forgive their father (or mother) or some other person who has hurt them.

Bill and I [Pam] have experienced much freedom in forgiveness. There are six basic principles, and if a person can walk her way through these six statements, she gains a handle on how to forgive in a tangible way. To move past a hurt (or a lifetime of them), write a list of all the people who have wounded you and what they did, then walk each through these Six Statements of Forgiveness as a prayer.

Simply pray, Lord:

1. I forgive [name the person] for [name the offense].
2. I admit that what was done was wrong.
3. I do not expect [person] to make up for what he has done.
4. I will not use this offense to define who [person] is.
5. I will not manipulate [person] with the offense.
6. I will not allow the offense to stop my growth.

These are all principles taken from what Jesus did on the cross for us. He knew our sins—each and every one of them—and He died for them. But to receive the benefit of Christ's death on the cross, we have to admit we are wrong. We have to repent. God wants us to forgive those who wounded us so we can be free to move forward in life, and be free to have healthy, whole relationships with others.

Be kind to one another, tender-hearted, forgiving each other, just as God in Christ also has forgiven you. (Ephesians 4:32, NASB)

Friendship Evaluation Worksheet

One of the most valuable possessions in life is having true friends. Learning how to be a good friend will equip you to choose positive, lasting friendships.

The Merriam-Webster Online Dictionary defines a *friend* as: "One attached to another by affection or esteem; a favored companion." In other words: A friend is someone you love (affection) and respect (esteem) and who is one of your favorite people (favored companion).

Most importantly, God's Word provides insight into friendships as well: *(Note: This is how God desires to see our friendships.)*

Romans 13:8 (TLB): "Pay all your debts except the debt of love for others [your friends]—Never finish paying that!"

Paul was writing to the Philippians when he instructed:

"Fulfill my joy by being like-minded, having the same love, being of one accord [in agreement together, being in unity], of one mind." (Philippians 2:2, NKJV)

Following is a simple worksheet for you to fill out:

Circle below the qualities below that are most important to you in a friend.

Loyal	Trustworthy	Likes to party
Funny	Lets me be myself	Passionate for God
Compassionate	Honest	Generous
Patient	Enjoys other friends	Faithful

Dependable   Forgiving   Courageous
Understanding   Has a healthy, loving family Caring
Believes in me   Will defend me   Not jealous
Others qualities not listed:

_____

_____

To think about:

Are you the kind of friend that you look for in others?

If so, what are some of the qualities you offer to your friends?

_____

_____

_____

When you initiate friendships according to God's Word you begin to build a relationship by your common goals.

What are some things you have in common and similar goals you might share with a friend? (See the examples below.)

_____

_____

_____

Things in Common:

- Your parents are friends
- You attend the same church
- You live in the same neighborhood
- You both are in the same grade or attend the same school

Common Goals:

- Enjoy similar hobbies, clubs, or sports
- Work together on projects
- Complete a Bible study together
- Go on a mission trip together

If you have at least one thing in common and one common goal, and you both mutually respect and like each other, then you will likely build a close friendship.

Would you like a guarantee that what has begun in your friendships will grow and flourish for the rest of your life? I am about to give you a most powerful tool, the secret to a strong foundation for your friendships. With this tool you can proactively influence the direction you choose to go in, the choices you make, and the person you will become.

The answer: **Grow closer to Jesus together!** Do a Bible study together, go on a mission trip, serve in your church or community, feed the homeless—wherever you are, with Christ in mind, you'll find ways to be Jesus to each other and to others around you. And you'll be blessed to see your friendships grow stronger each time you are together.

Remember: "Friends come and friends go, but a true friend sticks by you like family" (Proverbs 18:24, MSG).

Compilation of this worksheet created and authored by
Naomi Shedd & Doreen Hanna (2009)

My Covenant with God
(for Princess to sign as she is ready)

I take God to be my Father; I take Jesus Christ to be my Savior.
I take the Holy Spirit to be my Guide. I take the Bible to be the rule
of my life. I take the Christian people to be my associates; I take
Christian work to be my duty. I likewise dedicate myself to the Lord,
and this I do freely, deliberately, sincerely, and forever.

Name _____

Date _____

Items to Ask For

Worksheet for those who are part of a non-profit organization or are doing a community outreach program for a group of girls.

The following recommendations are places to consider contacting because they may contribute their services or products simply because you are reaching out helping teen girls in your local community. If they say *yes* to your request, you in turn should offer to list their business on the back of your celebration program (that you pass out to everyone at the celebration) enabling them to receive free advertising for their contribution.

The following recommendations are based on a group of 12 girls.

Preparing for distribution of affirmation cards for Session 1:

Contact a local printing company. Ask for a several boxes of note cards (at least 48 cards and envelopes), also one box of envelopes (5"x 9" that contains 50); remember, each smaller note card and envelope will go in the larger envelope.

Sessions 2, 3, 4:

Request from your local office supplies store a package of plain certificates. You will fill out the certificates by writing the meaning of each girl's first (and possibly her middle) name, and then present it to her at these sessions. You may also want to ask for note cards that will be given to the parents, including step-in dads (a box of 25 cards or two boxes of 12 each—one more feminine, the other masculine).

Session 6:

Contact a beauty consultant or a makeup artist who would be willing to come and give basic instruction on facial cleansing and then provide a makeover for each girl with an emphasis on enhancing their natural beauty. Also, locate a woman who would be willing to offer appropriate etiquette instruction (such as setting a table for a fine-dining meal and learning the suitable manners that are required for such an occasion). Ask a local restaurant or caterer to donate the meal for the luncheon or dinner where the instruction will take place.

Session 7:

Contact a local beauty store that will donate 12 mirrors and/or samples of makeup.

Celebration needs:
- A local food store to donate items for appetizers and/or drinks
- A local bakery to donate the cake
- A party store that will donate the balloons and/or paper goods
- A local coffee place to donate the coffee and tea
- A florist shop that will donate bouquets
- A photographer who will donate his or her time to take pictures of each girl and the event

Remember: Each encounter gives you the opportunity to demonstrate God's love and also build relationships in your community. Be sure to extend the invitation for the donors to attend this celebration. Don't forget to send a thank-you card!

"My Favorites" Worksheet

Name: _____

My Favorite Flower: _____

My Favorite Thing in Nature: (The ocean, the moon, the stars, a river, a mountain, etc.) _____

_____

_____

My Favorite Animal and Why: _____

_____

_____

_____

My Favorite Food: _____

_____

_____

My Favorite Place to Go: _____

_____

_____

Imparting a Blessing

Give a *Meaningful Touch*. A kiss or hug or laying on of hands. (Demonstrates warmth, personal acceptance, and affirmation.)

Give a *Verbal Acknowledgment*. "The tongue has the power of life and death" (Proverbs 18:21). A blessing imparts life and hope for the future,

_____

_____

_____

_____

_____

_____

_____

Attach *High Value*, connecting her character to a word picture.

Use an everyday object—for example, an animal, something in nature, and so on. Match the positive attributes of the object to those you see in her.

(Example: "I see you as a bird—free, graceful, gentle, and admired by others." Or, "I see you like a mighty oak tree—well founded, bold and strong.")

Picture her potential future. What do you see her becoming?

_____

_____

_____

_____

_____

_____

Choose a scripture that you believe is applicable to her life.

_____

_____

_____

_____

_____

_____

(Adapted and Excerpted from *The Gift of the Blessing*)

Sample "Night of Celebration" Request for Help

We respectfully request your assistance in making this celebration a success for everyone. You can help by volunteering to assist in the following areas. Please put your name and phone number next to the area you would like to assist in.

Provide Decorations: _____

Provide the Cake: _____

Provide Drinks: _____

Provide Paper Goods: _____

Provide Appetizers: _____

Provide Bouquets for Daughters: _____

Need cash contributions for cameraman: $100 (can be divided between two or more families) _____

Honorarium for Pastor: $50 _____

If you have any suggestions or questions please call:

_____

Thank you in advance for making your daughter's
"Night of Celebration" a lasting memory.

FOCUS ON THE FAMILY®

Welcome to the Family

Whether you purchased this book, borrowed it, or received it as a gift, we're glad you're reading it. It's just one of the many helpful, encouraging, and biblically based resources produced by Focus on the Family® for people in all stages of life.

Focus began in 1977 with the vision of one man, Dr. James Dobson, a licensed psychologist and author of numerous best-selling books on marriage, parenting, and family. Alarmed by the societal, political, and economic pressures that were threatening the existence of the American family, Dr. Dobson founded Focus on the Family with one employee and a once-a-week radio broadcast aired on 36 stations.

Now an international organization reaching millions of people daily, Focus on the Family is dedicated to preserving values and strengthening and encouraging families through the life-changing message of Jesus Christ.

Focus on the Family MAGAZINES

These faith-building, character-developing publications address the interests, issues, concerns, and challenges faced by every member of your family from preschool through the senior years.

FOCUS ON THE FAMILY® MAGAZINE	FOCUS ON THE FAMILY CLUBHOUSE JR.® Ages 4 to 8	FOCUS ON THE FAMILY CLUBHOUSE® Ages 8 to 12	FOCUS ON THE FAMILY CITIZEN® U.S. news issues

For More INFORMATION

ONLINE:
Log on to
FocusOnTheFamily.com
In Canada, log on to
FocusOnTheFamily.ca

PHONE:
Call toll-free:
800-A-FAMILY
(232-6459)
In Canada, call toll-free:
800-661-9800

Rev. 12/08

More Great Resources
from Focus on the Family®

Raising a Modern-Day Knight
By Robert Lewis

The medieval custom of knighthood offers a unique approach to shaping a boy into a strong, godly man. Centuries ago, select boys went through a rigorous, years-long process of clearly defined objectives, goals, and ceremonies—with the hope of achieving knighthood. Along the way, they acquired a boldly masculine vision, an uncompromising code of conduct, and a noble cause in which to invest their lives. They were the heroes of their age.

In much the same way, *Raising a Modern-Day Knight* will show how you, too, can confidently guide your son to the kind of authentic, biblical manhood that can change our world.

Beauty Secrets
By Dr. Deborah Newman & Rachel Newman
Girls can choose self-acceptance over slavery to "beauty."

Dr. Deborah Newman, who has spent over 18 years as a counselor, has heard too many sad stories of body bashing and self-depreciation. In this book, she and her teen daughter, Rachel, share beauty secrets that are always in style—regardless of current makeover trends and "ideals." *Beauty Secrets* arms young women with the truth from God's Word and a fresh perspective on genuine beauty and self-worth.

Mother & Daughter: Closer to God and to Each Other
By Susie Shellenberger

Take one part talking, two parts listening, sprinkle liberally with Scripture and fun activities and what do you have? Susie Shellenberger's book *Closer*, written especially for mothers and teen daughters to experience together. *Closer* includes questions that reveal the hearts of moms and daughters to each other, scriptures that explore life, and prayers to pray.

FOR MORE INFORMATION
Online:
Log on to FocusOnTheFamily.com
In Canada, log on to focusonthefamily.ca.

Phone:
Call toll free: 800-A-FAMILY
In Canada, call toll free: 800-661-9800.

FOCUS®
ON THE FAMILY

BPZZXP1

Focus on the Family®
Presents

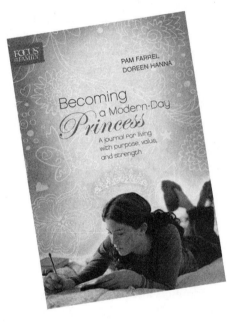

Equip your daughter with her very own *Becoming a Modern-Day Princess* journal. This fun and useful journal, by Pam Farrel and Doreen Hanna, provides a place for girls to write out their thoughts and work through their feelings as they receive advice on relevant issues, such as transitioning to womanhood, finding identity in Christ, friendships, guys, and so much more!

Order at FocusOnTheFamily.com/resources
or call 1(800)A-Family (232-6459).

About the Authors

Pam and Bill Farrel are international speakers, relationship experts on marriage and parenting, and the authors of more than 30 books, including the best-selling *Men Are Like Waffles, Women Are Like Spaghetti* and *The 10 Best Decisions Every Parent Can Make*. Pam is also the founder and president of *Seasoned Sisters*, an organization designed to encourage and equip women forty and beyond. For more information, go to www.seasonedsisters.com. Pam and Bill have ongoing relationship columns in magazines and newspapers, are frequent guests on radio and TV, and their resources have been translated into more than 15 languages. Pam and Bill also have experience as a pastoral couple and are available for speaking engagements. They have parented three children and enjoy their relationship with their daughter-in-law and granddaughter.

To contact the Farrels:
Farrel Communications
3755 Avocado Blvd. #414
La Mesa, CA 91941
(800) 810-4449
www.farrelcommunications.com

❦

Doreen Hanna is the founder and president of Treasured Celebrations Ministries. She is passionate about empowering men and women of all ages to live a blessed and adventurous life. She's a national motivational speaker and was one of Women of Faith's first National Field Representatives, emceeing many of their pre-conference events. For more than 25 years, Doreen has been a Bible study teacher and counselor to women. She was a contributing author in *Families Can Bounce Back, Refined By Fire* and *Women Mentoring Women*. She and her husband, Chad, live in beautiful Santa Fe, New Mexico. They have two daughters and two granddaughters, who are the ultimate highlight to grandparenthood.

To contact Doreen:
Treasured Celebrations Ministries
7608 Cree Circle
Santa Fe, NM 87507
505-424-0522
www.doreenhanna.org